THE HISTORY OF THE FORMULA E

Race to race

Chad miller

All rights reserved 2021

Any form of reproduction of this work, in whole or in part, without the express consent of its author, in any graphic, electronic or mechanical means, including photocopying or recording or any other information retrieval and storage system, is prohibited.

Cover graphic resources: audi-mediacenter.com / movilidadelectrica.com/dsautomobiles.ps

INTRODUCTION

The future of motorsports is electric. And Formula E brings the future to the present. It is, without a doubt, the most futuristic speed competition with the most developed technology. Its main attraction is seeing those almost sci-fi-looking cars racing with that classic movie starship sound.

Although it is also true that it has had to mature enough to become what it is today. The first years were difficult, with cars that still did not meet the expectations of the brands or the fans. This was resolved with continuous improvements in power and batteries, and with the inclusion of the Gen2, the current single-seater and that in the near future will be replaced by the Gen3.

This attracted more powerful manufacturers, and both BMW and more recently Porsche and the almighty Mercedes have ended up joining this adventure that improves season by season. That is why it is interesting to know the history of the competition, because it is impossible to enjoy Formula E to the fullest without having known its development.

In addition, remembering its history is enjoying the great battles between Audi and Renault, between Buemi and di Grassi… and the equality in the category that allows unexpected and surprising results, something that is longed for in the main automobile competitions. Let's not forget that all Formula E teams share a chassis for this purpose.

Thus, the objective of this book is twofold: on the one hand, to remember the exciting past struggles, and on the other hand that you can approach the competition so that you can enjoy it in its entirety, as an expert and thus be able to add the incredible Formula E to the list of automobile competitions that make you enjoy.

I hope these pages are to your liking and are useful to you.

Extraconfidencial.com

March 3, 2011: the origin of it all

Formula E was organized in an informal dinner on March 3, 2011 in an Italian restaurant in Paris, at a table where they shared a pleasant evening the president of the FIA Jean Todt, the Spanish businessman Alejandro Agag, the Italian politician Antonio Tajani and also Italian actor Teo Teocoli. With such a representation, something great had to come out of that encounter.

In this way, the proposal to create a motorsport championship with electric single-seaters was presented. Tajani emphasized the need to encourage the electrification of the automobile industry and Agag would take charge of bringing the show to life by seeking sponsors, hiring televisions and handling marketing.

Thus, in that meeting the foundations were laid for the creation of the electric single-seater championship that would end up being called Formula E.

The proposal began to materialize as the various teams, with an interest in promoting the electric future of the brands, joined the championship. For the first edition, the participation of up to 10 different teams was obtained:

- ✓ Virgin Racing (UK)
- ✓ Mahindra Racing (India)
- ✓ Dragon Racing (USA)
- ✓ Renault e.Dams (France)
- ✓ Trulli (Switzerland)
- ✓ Audi Sport ABT Schaeffler (Germany)
- ✓ Venturi (Monaco)
- ✓ Andretti (USA)
- ✓ Amlin Aguri (Japan)
- ✓ China Racing (China), which throughout the season would be renamed NEXTEV TCR.

With the foundations settled and the commitment of a dozen teams, everything was ready to organize the first edition of the championship.

It only remained to get the most important element: the electric car that would represent the competition.

Motorafondo.net

Spark-Renault SRT 01E: the first single-seater

For the competition, it was agreed that all teams would use the same car, designed by Fréderic Vasseur. This essentially made it possible to save costs, avoiding that each team had to develop its own, thus sharing development and research expenses. In addition, this would allow greater equality on the track, a feature that was being missed the most in Formula 1. Sharing a car would give all the teams the opportunity to win and thus the drivers would compete on equal terms, creating more exciting races where they did not. the probable winner was known before its start.

The chassis of the first car was developed jointly by Spark Racing Technology and Dallara. It used an engine provided by Mclaren and the tires were from the Michelin brand. The battery, a key element in the competition, was manufactured by Williams.

Turbosquid.com

The Renault-Spark SRT 01E had 250 horsepower, could accelerate from 0 to 100 km / h in 3 seconds and reach a top speed of 225 km / h.

One of the most striking characteristics at the beginning of the competition was that the batteries did not have the necessary capacity to power the car throughout the entire race. This forced the drivers ... to change cars in the middle of the competition, in a somewhat peculiar image that detracted from the electrical capabilities of the car, and that it would be urgent to solve as soon as possible.

Motorpasion.com

The great prizes of Formula E were called ePrix, and these take place in urban environments, with paths characterized by having great braking and deceleration in order to favor the recharging of the battery.

These are circuits created on the streets of the cities themselves. The first cities to host this type of event were Beijing, Monaco, Moscow, Berlin, Putrajaya, Punta del Este, London, Buenos Aires, Miami and Long Beach.

Monkeymotor.net

In this way, and with everything already prepared, on September 13, 2014 these new high-pitched and futuristic-sounding cars began to compete in Beijing.

Rallystar.net

SEASON 2014-2015

Beijing ePrix

The first driver to secure pole position for an ePrix was French driver Nicolas Prost, son of four-time Formula 1 champion Alain Prost. He did it with the Renault e.Dams team. Prost had become a tester for the Renault Formula 1 team between 2010 and 2014, however, he failed to gain a foothold in the team, so he decided to try his luck in Formula E.

Revistasafetycar.com

Nicolas Prost led the entire first race of Formula E, except for one lap after his stop to change vehicles, until the last corner ... Nick Heidfeld, who was driving for Venturi, had been closing the gap with Prost on the last leg of the race So in the last corner he tried to pass him to get the victory. Prost caused an overtaking collision that sent Heidfeld flying into the barriers. The Frenchman apologized to Heidfeld for subsequently hitting him.

Motor.es

With the first two positioned out of the fight, Lucas di Grassi took the opportunity to clinch the first victory in a Formula E race, with the Audi Sport ABT team.

Hibridosyelectricos.com

Di Grassi, in addition to Bruno Senna and the British pilot Katherine Legge, had the help of the Fanboost in this first race. This is an additional power that they can use for five seconds in the second half of the race and that is achieved through a vote of the fans. The fans of the competition can vote to choose their favorite pilots and that three of them receive this energy boost. With it, the competition seeks to enable spectators to decide and actively participate in the races.

However, none of the three decided to use this aid considering that it breaks the equality, which made the organization force it to be used from the second race of the season.

Second was the Swiss Sébastien Buemi with the other Renault e.Dams, while third was Daniel Abt with the other Audi, although later he was sanctioned for using more electrical power than allowed, which allowed Sam Bird and his team to get on the podium. Virgin Racing team.

After this first race, it was concluded that Renault e.Dams and Audi Sport were the teams that started the championship with the most force. Mahindra Racing was able to place Karun Chandhok in fifth position and Dragon Racing allowed Belgian Jérome D'Ambrosio to finish sixth, followed by Andretti's two French drivers: Franck Montagny and Charles Pic.

Putrajaya ePrix

After the first test in China, the championship moved to Malaysia for its second race. The event had to be delayed for a little over a month at the request of the country's prime minister, and the time also had to be advanced due to the forecast of heavy rains.

In any case, the race started with the Spanish Oriol Servià from pole with the North American Dragon Team. Bruno Senna and Katherine Legge once again had the extra power by popular vote of the Fanboost, in addition to Nick Heidfeld.

The victory in Malaysia went to British Sam Bird, from the Virgin Racing team. Before coming to Formula E, Bird had been runner-up in the GP2 Series and third in Formula Renault 3.5. Starting in 2014, he combined Formula E with the FIA World Endurance Championship (in which he would become champion in 2015 in the LMP2 class and runner-up in 2016 in the LMGTE Pro).

Motoresapleno.com.ar

Second was Brazilian Lucas di Grassi, who continued to show Audi's potential, followed by the two Renault e.Dams drivers. Buemi was third and Prost was fourth, a great result considering that the Swiss was penalized in qualifying for not meeting the weight limit in the car and Prost was penalized with ten positions at the start for causing the collision with Heidfeld in Beijing .

After the Malaysian race, the top two drivers in the standings were di Grassi with 43 points and Sam Bird with 40. In terms of teams, Audi led with 45 points with Virgin Racing stuck with 44.

However, the real threat seemed to be Renault e.Dams, which despite accumulated penalties from its drivers and incidents, had 33 points in third place.

Punta del Este ePrix

The third race of the first season was held in Uruguay. In it, three pilots abandoned the championship: Franck Montagny, Ho-Ping Tung and Katherine Legge, and were replaced by Antonio García, Salvador Durán and Jean-Éric Vergne. These last two, together with Heidfeld, achieved the third Fanboost of the season.

The Frenchman Vergne could not make a better debut, getting pole position. However, in the closing stages of a bumpy race with three safety cars, he was second behind Buemi. Vergne tried to overtake the Swiss using the Fanboost, but it was not enough. Then, under pressure, Buemi skipped a chicane in which it was debated whether he should surrender his first position for it, but the dilemma ended when Vergne had to retire for breaking the suspension with two laps to go and after a great debut.

Thus, Sébastien Buemi claimed victory for a Renault e.Dams team that dominated the championship. The Swiss driver had raced for three years in Formula 1 with Toro Rosso without great success before moving on to the World Endurance Championship with Toyota and combining it with Formula E.

Infopits.mx

Second was Nelson Piquet Jr. for China Racing and third was Lucas di Grassi for Audi, enough for the Brazilian to maintain the lead with a slight advantage over Buemi and Bird.

In terms of teams, e.Dams was unsurprisingly leading, just two points ahead of Audi. Virgin Racing was third now.

Buenos Aires ePrix

The World Cup moved to Argentina in its next race, to the city of Buenos Aires, where Heidfeld, Vergne and Senna were the favorites of the fans to get extra power.

Buemi continued with his good result in Uruguay, achieving pole position, and in the first part of the race he was attacked by Heidfeld who could not overtake him even with the use of the Fanboost.

For his part, di Grassi rallied to second place and became Buemi's main threat. However, they both erred in strategy when after Karun Chandhok's accident, after deploying the safety car, they entered the pits one lap late. However, after a lot of confusion, the cars were restructured again allowing the vehicles behind the safety car to rejoin and Buemi and di Grassi once again returned to the top positions.

With 13 laps to go, Buemi hit the wall, breaking the suspension and thus losing his possible victory. Di Grassi, who then led the event, suffered the same fate: suspension break and retirement.

Heidfeld then led the race for Venturi, but was then penalized for speeding on pit road.

Therefore, the Portuguese António Félix da Costa of the Amlin Aguri team remained leader of the race until the end, although a few minutes before he had no great chances of victory, he achieved the victory in Argentina. The Portuguese driver had been a Red Bull tester and had competed in several races in the DTM before moving on to Formula E.

Revistadelmotor.es

In this exciting race with an unexpected finish, Nicolas Prost was second and saved the Renault e.Dams points, while Nelson Piquet Jr. again achieved a great result for China Racing on the podium.

Despite bad luck, di Grassi held the lead 10 points ahead of Sam Bird.

Renault e.Dams also held the team lead, 9 points behind Virgin Racing which rose to second place while Audi fell to third.

Miami ePrix

The fifth round of the championship was in the United States, on the streets of Miami. This time again three riders were out of the competition without having had a great success in it: Oriol Servià, Marco Andretti and Michela Cerrutti. Their places were taken by Loïc Duval, Scott Speed and Vitantonio Liuzzi. Salvador Durán, Vergne and Bruno Senna were the fan favorites this time.

Jean-Éric Vergne achieved a pole that he could not use after being out of the race due to a collision. Instead, it was Nicolas Prost who managed to clinch the victory, who had had a great start to the championship despite several incidents, which was another victory for a Renault e.Dams that continued to prove themselves as the strongest team.

Tobiteve.com

Second was the rookie Scott Speed, the American managed to get on the podium in his first race with the Venturi team. The podium was completed by Daniel Abt for an Audi team that seemed to regain its good feeling at the start of the championship.

Di Grassi was 11th, which meant he lost the lead to Nicolas Prost. In terms of teams, e.Dams held the top position, and Audi beat Virgin to regain second place.

Long Beach ePrix

The sixth race of the season was also in the United States, in this case at Long Beach. The drivers most voted by fans were Piquet Jr., Vergne and Sam Bird.

Daniel Abt, after his third place in Miami, continued in good shape taking pole in Long Beach, although he would have complications finally finishing in 15th position.

The driver who achieved victory was Nelson Piquet Jr., with a China Racing that managed to achieve sporadic successes. Nelsinho, the son of three-time Formula 1 champion Nelson Piquet, had raced for two years with Renault in F1 with not very successful results and a controversial finish. After participating in several NASCAR categories, in Formula E he was beginning to find his place.

Motoresapleno.com.ar

Second was Jean-Éric Vergne who finally managed to materialize his efforts in a great result for Andretti, and the podium was completed by di Grassi for Audi, who added some very important points for both the drivers 'and teams' championships. Buemi, fourth, saved a few points for e.Dams.

Di Grassi regained the leadership of the drivers' championship just one point above Piquet in a magnificent duel between the Brazilians.

For its part, e.Dams continued with a comfortable lead over Audi, followed by Virgin Racing and Andretti.

Monaco ePrix

The Principality of Monaco hosted the seventh race of the first season, where Piquet, Vergne and Durán obtained the best popular vote.

Buemi took pole followed by di Grassi to add more excitement to the battle between Renault e.Dams and Audi. The fight in qualifying moved to the race, keeping the same positions when crossing the finish line, so the Swiss achieved victory in the streets of Monaco.

Diariomotor.com

Nelson Piquet achieved third place for China Racing, which was renamed NEXTEV TCR.

With these results, di Grassi kept the lead only 4 points ahead of Piquet who accumulated 89, and joined the fight for the title Buemi with 83 points.

Buemi's victory allowed Renault e.Dams to lead the championship even further, 45 points above Audi, while Virgin held third place ahead of NEXTEV TCR.

Berlin ePrix

The eighth test took place in Germany, on a runway built for the occasion near the Berlin airport. The 30 kilowatts of the Fanboost lead were given to Piquet, Buemi and Charles Pic.

Jarno Trulli took pole and defended the first position against Buemi, who managed to pass him in the third corner after sliding the rear of the Italian's car.

Jérome d'Ambrosio surprised with a great change of vehicle during the stops that helped him to put himself in second position behind di Grassi, although afterwards he was not able to keep up with the Brazilian who ended up winning the race.

However, Audi could not celebrate the victory as scrutineering after the race showed that di Grassi's vehicle had unauthorized modifications to the wing, on a chassis that was common and shared by all teams by regulation. Di Grassi was disqualified and d'Ambrosio became the Berlin champion with Dragon Racing. The Belgian had driven for a year in the Marussia Formula 1 team in 2011 before competing in Formula E.

Infoauto.com.ar

Second was Buemi, who after di Grassi's disqualification, added some very important points for the drivers' championship. Third was the other Dragon Racing driver, Loïc Duval, who made the North American team achieve a great result in Berlin.

The penalty dropped di Grassi to third in the drivers' standings, while Piquet took the opportunity to take the lead over Buemi.

Renault e.Dams maintained its comfortable first position in the team classification, while Dragon Racing surprised by reaching second place, a point above Audi that lost a great opportunity with the disqualification of di Grassi.

Moscow ePrix

The penultimate round of the championship was held in Russia, where the results were beginning to be decisive. Piquet, Buemi and di Grassi, who were competing for the drivers' title, received the Fanboost on this occasion.

The Frenchman Jean-Éric Vergne got a pole again... that he could not take advantage of in the race finishing it in fourth place.

The battle for the Russian ePrix, which extended to the drivers' championship, was between two Brazilians: Nelson Piquet Jr. and Lucas di Grassi, the former winning. Piquet secured the victory for NEXTEV, thus increasing their advantage in the classification and increasing their morale for the final part of the championship.

Autobild.es

Nick Heidfeld, always in the top positions, but without finishing big wins, managed to complete the podium for Venturi. For his part, Buemi finished ninth, complicating the fight for the championship.

With only the London double date to finish the championship, Piquet led the drivers' championship with 128 points, followed by di Grassi with 111. Somewhat behind, although still with mathematical options, Buemi was in third position with 105 points.

The poor result of the Renault e.Dams drivers in Moscow (Nicolas Prost was eighth), kept the leading team but only 44 points ahead of Audi thanks to di Grassi's second place, and he could not relax yet. Piquet's victory put NEXTEV TCR third, 11 points behind Audi.

London ePrix 1

The season ended in London with a double date, two races that would end up determining the first Formula E champion, in a rather tight fight between Piquet, di Grassi and Buemi with a slight advantage for the first. As for the teams, while Renault e.Dams was the clear favorite to win the title, there could still be some surprises.

In this last round of the championship there were up to four driver changes: Jaime Alguersuari (due to health problems), Vitantonio Liuzzi, Justin Wilson and Charles Pic left, being replaced by Fabio Leimer, Alex Fontana, Simona de Silvestro and Oliver Turvey.

Buemi achieved pole, with di Grassi third and Piquet fourth, which gave the Swiss some hope to surprise and end up becoming champion. Buemi took advantage of the opportunity and ended up winning the race.

Diariomotor.com

Their rivals finished one position behind what they had qualified: di Grassi fourth and Piquet fifth. This made Piquet remain the leader of the standings, but now only 5 points ahead of Buemi, who in turn surpassed di Grassi by 8 points.

D'Ambrosio achieved a great second place for Dragon Racing while the podium was completed by Vergne for Andretti.

London ePrix 2

After the first race in London, the classification had been even more equal, which made us look forward to an exciting final race. Buemi was only 5 points behind Piquet. In addition, he had the advantage of having been the fastest on the circuit where the decisive race was to take place. Di Grassi, who had lagged behind, also had options to be proclaimed champion.

The team championship, after Buemi's victory, was already sentenced. Renault e.Dams was 64 points ahead of Audi that could no longer recover, so the French team thus became the first team to win a Formula E championship.

Group.renault.com

With the drivers' title still to be resolved, Stéphane Sarrazin surprised by taking pole for Venturi in the second London race.

The best classified of the protagonists in the fight for the drivers' title was Buemi... in sixth position. Di Grassi was 11th and Piquet 16th. The Brazilians would have to improve in the race if they wanted to avoid Buemi's triumph.

Buemi could not be as fast as in the first race in London, and finished in fifth position, with which he added 10 points. Di Grassi was sixth, scoring 8 points, which kept him behind Buemi.

As for Piquet ... he finished the race in seventh position, scoring 6 points, four less than Buemi, which meant that with the five advantage with which he faced the last race, it was enough for the Brazilian to be proclaimed as the first champion Formula E with just one point advantage in an exciting season finale.

Jakartaglobe.id

FINAL CLASSIFICATION 2014-2015

Nelson Piquet Jr.	144	Renault e.Dams	232
Sébastien Buemi	143	Dragon Racing	171
Lucas di Grassi	133	Audi Sport ABT	165
Jérome D'Ambrosio	113	NEXTEV TCR	152
Sam bird	103	Virgin racing	133
Nicolas Prost	89	Andretti	119
Jean-Éric Vergne	70	Amlin aguri	66
António Felix da Costa	51	Mahindra Racing	58
Loïc Duval	42	Venturi	53
Bruno senna	40	Trulli	17
Daniel Abt	32		
Nick heidfeld	31		
Jaime Alguersuari	30		
Stéphan Sarrazin	22		
Scott speed	18		
Franck montagny	18		
Karun Chandhok	18		
Charles pic	16		
Oriol Servià	16		
Jarno trulli	15		
Salvador Duran	13		
Oliver Turvey	4		
Vitantonio Liuzzi	2		
Takuma Sato	2		
Justin wilson	1		
Ho-Pin Tung	0		
Simona de Silvestro	0		
Antonio Garcia	0		
Michela Cerruti	0		
Marco Andretti	0		
Matthew brabham	0		
Fabio Lemer	0		
Alex Fontana	0		
Katherine Legge	0		
Sakon yamamoto	0		

Motorsportcars.es

2015-2016: Second season, with development of power units

The success of the first season allowed Formula E to continue to develop and grow in a new edition. In this second campaign, the main characteristic was that each team had the freedom to develop its own power unit.

Virtually all teams decided to develop their own electric motor, while Team Aguri opted to use the one from the previous season. Dragon Racing reached an agreement with Venturi to use the same power unit, while the Trulli team, due to problems in the development of the engine, decided to withdraw from the competition. Having been in last position the previous season, the team ended their adventure in Formula E.

The maximum power use throughout the race was also changed, from 150 kilowatts (200 horsepower) to 170 kilowatts (230 horsepower). All of this made us expect a new season even more surprising than the first.

As for the leading drivers of the first season, they remained in their respective teams. Sébastien Buemi and Nicolas Prost repeated with

Renault e.Dams. Lucas di Grassi and Daniel Abt were also confirmed at Audi. Piquet continued on NEXTEV TCR, this time alongside a full season of Oliver Turvey.

Thus, without much more news except for the change of some team name due to sponsorships, the second season of Formula E began.

Beijing ePrix

The championship started again for the second time in China. In this race, three drivers made their debut: Jacques Villeneuve with Venturi, Nathanaël Berton with Team Aguri and Robin Frijns with Andretti (who was renamed Amlin Andretti for sponsorship reasons). The three drivers chosen by the fans for the Fanboost were Piquet, Sam Bird and Oliver Turvey.

Buemi took pole showing that he and his team were still strong in the championship. Heidfeld, after a great start in which he took second place, attacked Buemi in the first part of the race without success.

Buemi ended up comfortably winning the first race of the season, and di Grassi finished second without much difficulty as well, in what looked like it was starting to be a repeat of the previous year.

Diariomotor.com

Heidfeld, despite the difficulties, managed to retain the podium. The two Dragon Racing drivers, Loïc Duval and Jérome d'Ambrosio, achieved a creditable fourth and fifth place thanks to the strategy of changing vehicles late to reach the finish with more energy. The champion, Piquet, with many problems was doubled twice and did not start the championship in very good condition.

Putrajaya ePrix

In the second season, the championship also returned to Malaysia. Buemi achieved his second consecutive pole and was beginning to dominate the championship.

However, this time he was unable to turn pole into victory, finishing 12th, which together with Nicolas Prost's 10th place was a not very beneficial ePrix for the champion team.

The victory went to di Grassi who achieved the victory for Audi, a team renamed ABT Schaeffler Audi Sport.

Motoryracing.com

With only two races contested, it could be sensed that the battle for the title would be between Buemi and di Grassi, since Piquet only managed to be eighth in Malaysia.

Second was Sam Bird for Virgin and Dutch Robin Frijns completed the podium for Amlin Andretti.

Punta del Este ePrix

Uruguay once again hosted the third race in the second season. Oliver Rowland replaced Heifeld, who had injured his wrist in the previous race.

The Dragon Racing of Jérome d'Ambrosio and Loïc Duval surprised by being the fastest in a classification in which Jacques Villeneuve had an accident that prevented him from participating later in the race as he did not have time to repair the vehicle.

The Dragons failed to maintain the lead, dropping to third and fourth at the end of the race.

The first two were expected, with Buemi being the first to cross the finish line ahead of di Grassi.

Autobild.es

With three races contested, Buemi led the championship with a single point of advantage over di Grassi in what was beginning to be a very intense and even fight, well above the rest of the drivers.

As for the teams, something similar happened: Renault e.Dams held the first position only 2 points above Audi, and already more than 20 points above Dragon Racing.

Buenos Aires ePrix

Argentina repeated in the championship and in Buenos Aires the fourth round of the championship was held. Villeneuve, after a not very successful stint in Formula E, left the competition and was replaced in the Venturi team by Mike Conway. Salvador Durán returned with the Team Aguri team. The fan favorites this time were Vergne, Bird and di Grassi.

Sam Bird took pole for Virgin Racing, followed by Nicolas Prost for Renault e.Dams. Of the drivers fighting for the championship, di Grassi came seventh, and Buemi... last.

After an erratic qualifying, Buemi achieved a great comeback in the race, worthy of a champion, and even surpassed di Grassi. Buemi was second, getting some advantage in this particular fight, while the Brazilian was third.

Lalasport.com

Meanwhile and oblivious to the leadership struggle, Briton Sam Bird got the victory for DS Virgin Racing and was close to the leaders of the table, although still far behind them. The English driver, after being runner-up in GP2 in 2013, made the leap to the World Endurance Championship, being champion of the LMP2 category in 2015, while combining his participation in Formula E.

Diariomotor.com

Mexico City ePrix

For the fifth race, the World Cup moved to Mexico City. Without changes of drivers, the pole went to the Belgian Jérome d'Ambrosio, with di Grassi third and Buemi fifth in the fight for the championship.

This time it was the Brazilian who achieved the victory in the race. Jérome d'Ambrosio confirmed his good pace in qualifying by sneaking between the leader and Buemi, who finished third, which meant that di Grassi would have achieved a great result in Mexico... if scrutineering hadn't disqualified the Audi driver.

Di Grassi's car did not reach the minimum weight established by the regulations, which is why once again the Brazilian driver was penalized losing all his points. In this way, the Mexican victory happened to be for Jérome d'Ambrosio and for a Dragon Racing team that, without being able to compete in general with Audi or Renault, achieved good results.

Racing5.cl

The elimination of di Grassi gave an advantage to Buemi, who held the first position with 22 points of advantage over di Grassi. In fact, the Brazilian was closer to third place, Sam Bird, than to the leader.

In terms of teams, Renault e.Dams led with 136 points over Dragon Racing which placed second with 102. The disqualification of Audi lowered it to third place with 92 points.

Long Beach ePrix

With only one North American event this season, the World Cup held its sixth event in Long Beach.

The pole was obtained by António Félix da Costa for Team Aguri, however, he came out last in the race after detecting an illegal pressure in his tires. This allowed Sam Bird with his Virgin to start from the top position.

Bird lost the top position when on lap 12 he was overtaken by di Grassi, who held on to the end, even behind a safety car, to claim victory in the United States.

Carros.entravision.com

Frenchman Stéphane Sarrazin was second for Venturi, and the podium was completed by Daniel Abt, in a very beneficial day for Audi that was recovering especially after the moral blow received in Mexico by the disqualification of di Grassi.

Buemi, meanwhile, in an attempt to overtake Frijns, hit the Dutchman by climbing on top of him, losing the front wing. Both received an orange flag, being forced to repair their vehicles, and the Swiss also, because he was considered the cause of the accident, suffered a penalty that left him with no options to score in the race.

This allowed di Grassi to regain the top spot in the championship with a one-point lead over Buemi, while Sam Bird, 30 points behind the leader, still had some option to join the fight.

Audi also saw its position improved, regaining second place, just 6 points behind e.Dams and pushing the standings very tight.

Paris ePrix

Paris debuted in the championship in the seventh round of the season.

Sam Bird took pole in an attempt to stay in the race for the drivers' championship, but was overtaken by di Grassi early in the race. The Brazilian managed to finish the test first and extended his streak by achieving victory in France.

Motoryracing.com

Vergne took second place for Virgin, relegating Buemi to third place, completing the podium and trying to avoid as much loss of points as possible.

However, di Grassi achieved a further advantage in the standings in Paris, now 11 points ahead of the Swiss.

Audi was a little closer to Renault e.Dams in the team standings, separated by just 7 points and confirming once again as the top two teams in the championship.

Berlin ePrix

With only three races to go, the stakes were high in Germany and any poor result could leave drivers and teams without much aspiration to fight for the titles.

Vergne got pole, but the first position lasted only until the first corner, where he was overtaken by Buemi. From there, the Swiss dominated the race to claim another victory and prevent di Grassi from wandering off in the championship.

Racefans.net

The two Audi drivers completed the podium, with Daniel Abt in second position and di Grassi in third. Fourth was the other Renault e.Dams driver, Nicolas Prost, showing the passionate fight between the two teams throughout the season.

The victory left Buemi one point behind di Grassi, already with a Sam Bird with no options to join the battle. Renault, for its part, finished with a 13-point advantage over Audi in the absence of the last double event of the championship.

London ePrix 1

As in the inaugural season, the championship ended with a double race in London. With the two titles to be defined, no more emotion could be asked for the last date of the competition.

Nicolas Prost took pole position in the first race, predicting a good finish for Renault e.Dams. As for the drivers' fight, di Grassi came 11th and Buemi 14th.

Both managed to improve their positions in the race, the Brazilian finishing 4th and the Swiss 5th, one behind the other and maintaining the even fight until the end.

Prost converted his pole into victory by taking first place in the first race.

Rs.recette.sbh.sx

Second was Bruno Senna for Mahindra Racing and third was Vergne for Virgin. Daniel Abt, meanwhile, had to retire, leaving Audi with virtually no options to fight for the teams title in the final race.

London ePrix 2

With the team championship declined for Renault e.Dams, the individual fight was still very close between Buemi and di Grassi.

Buemi, three points behind in the general classification, took pole, followed by his teammate Prost as squire, leaving di Grassi in third place, ensuring a great fight in the last race, with a small advantage for the Swiss.

Already in the race, the battle that was fought between them was extraordinary.

Di Grassi tried to overtake Buemi at the start to prevent him from escaping from the start. In the attempt to overtake, the Brazilian hit the Swiss from behind, causing both cars damaged and forced into the pits. There was speculation as to whether the accident was a race fight or intentional on the part of di Grassi.

Youtube.com

In any case, both riders were left with practically no scoring options and were even on points after the 3 points achieved by Buemi's pole. At that point in the race, di Grassi was champion by comparison of results.

The only option for Buemi was to get the fastest lap and score extra points for it. Di Grassi also opted for the same strategy, so the fight for the title... turned into a fight for the fastest lap. Ultimately it was Sébastien Buemi who achieved the fastest lap, thus proclaiming himself world champion in a surprising finish.

Snaplap.net

Buemi's victory further strengthened the leadership of Renault e.Dams, a team that achieved its second world title and continued as the only champion in the first two editions of Formula E.

FINAL CLASSIFICATION 2015-2016

Sébastien Buemi	155	Renault e.Dams	270
Lucas di Grassi	153	Audi Sport ABT	221
Nicolas Prost	115	DS Virgin Racing	144
Sam bird	88	Dragon Racing	143
Jérome d'Ambrosio	83	Mahindra Racing	105
Stéphane Sarrazin	70	Venturi	75
Daniel Abt	68	Andretti	49
Loïc Duval	60	Aguri	32
Jean-Éric Vergne	56	NEXTEV TCR	19
Nick heidfeld	53		
Bruno senna	52		
Robin frijns	40		
António Felix da Costa	28		
Oliver Turvey	11		
Nelson Piquet Jr.	8		
Mike conway	7		
Nathanaël Berthon	4		
Simona de Silvestro	4		
Ma Qing Hua	0		
Jacques villeneuve	0		
Oliver Rowland	0		
Salvador Duran	0		
René Rast	0		
Vitantonio Liuzzi	0		
Jarno trulli	0		

Pinterest.es

2016-2017: a third season with more power

After two satisfactory editions with good audience results, Formula E continued on its way to establish itself as one of the best motorsport championships.

Having survived two seasons built enough confidence to attract newcomers to the competition. Jaguar came together as a team, with the support of Williams. Aguri, second to last ranked in the previous season, was bought by China Media Capital, who renamed him Techeetah. Dragon Racing opted this season to develop its own power unit instead of using Venturi's.

However, the most significant change was the increased power of the single-seaters. Many fans had expected Formula E to be an electric Formula 1, comparable in terms of speed, and that required developing the power units progressively at least so that the differences were not so noticeable.

Thus, the regeneration power was raised from 100 to 150 kW, which made it possible to achieve an additional 67 hp. The batteries also increased in size by 30 kilos, which allowed them to accumulate more energy and be able to squeeze the maximum of power for longer.

Formulaelectivalibre.blogspot.com

The main protagonists of this season were expected to once again be Renault e.Dams and Audi. Both had their drivers, Buemi and Nicolas Prost in the French team, and di Grassi and Daniel Abt in the German.

Piquet, the first Formula E champion, also remained at NEXTEV TCR, now renamed NextEV NIO.

It remained to be seen if another team or driver could aspire to one of the two titles in this new edition.

Hong Kong ePrix

This third season did not open in Beijing, and it would not be the only one of the big changes in the calendar. The competition started not far away, in Hong Kong.

The first pole of the year went to Nelson Piquet Jr., who after a disappointing season as reigning champion, was starting in the best possible way to once again show himself as a candidate for the title. Second was his partner Oliver Turvey, in a surprising start for NextEV NIO.

The two team drivers managed to maintain their positions in a clean start, but... they did not manage to maintain them until the end. In a race with many incidents in which Piquet slightly lost control of his car to finish on the barrier, the Brazilian finally finished 11th and his teammate 8th.

It was not a good start to the season for Audi, both di Grassi and Daniel Abt were involved in the incidents and with an orange flag, they were forced to go through the pits to repair the damage, although the talented Brazilian managed to climb up to second position.

Better was Renault e.Dams, the two-time world champion and team to beat, as Buemi got the victory to start the season on the right foot and Nicolas Prost was fourth.

Scmp.com

German Nick Heidfeld claimed his third Formula E podium, which was a hopeful start for the former Formula 1 driver.

Marrakech ePrix

Also with a new location, the world championship held the second round of the season in Morocco. Sweden's Felix Rosenqvist, who made his debut in the competition, achieved pole position for Mahindra Racing.

The Swede made a good start and his first laps were exceptional, managing to get away from the rest of the drivers, despite reporting an error on his steering wheel that left him without information. Still, he managed to hold the lead for most of the race, but a premature pit stop to change cars forced him to reserve energy late, allowing Buemi to overtake him. So, he dedicated himself to fighting for second position but could not prevent Sam Bird from passing him, finishing third in a race that ended with Sébastien Buemi's second victory and in which it seemed that it was going to be an easy season for him to revalidate. title.

Zimbio.com

Buenos Aires ePrix

The third race was in Buenos Aires, a place already known for the Formula E championship. Pole went to di Grassi, just when Audi most needed to react so that Renault e.Dams did not monopolize the championship.

A problem with Adam Carroll's Jaguar forced the first lap on the yellow flag, so the race actually started in the second.

Di Grassi was unable to maintain the first position with a good attack from Vergne, after which he dedicated himself to maintaining the second place against Buemi, something that he could not finally achieve.

Once the second position was achieved, the Swiss launched himself in pursuit of Jean-Éric Vergne, whom he finally managed to overcome to achieve the third victory of the season and maintain the full triumphs.

Autobild.es

Buemi's three victories in three races put him in the lead with 75 points, followed by di Grassi with 46, who was finding it increasingly difficult to keep up with the Swiss.

The three victories of Buemi were reflected in the championship of teams with the leadership of Renault e.Dams with 111 points on the 60 of Audi. Behind, Mahindra surprised with the third position with 37 points.

Mexico City ePrix

With the absolute dominance of Buemi in the competition it was arrived at Mexico City.

Oliver Turvey took pole for NextEV NIO and held first place after the start. Meanwhile, Sarrazin collided with di Grassi, forcing the Brazilian into the pits.

Leader Turvey had power problems and was forced to stop the car, which caused the safety car to leave, a fact that benefited di Grassi who had already made the stop and allowed him to take first position, although he would arrive with less energy to the final part of the race. Despite this inconvenience, the Brazilian managed to become the winner of the test, a very remarkable result considering that his main rival, Buemi, could only finish 14th.

Polepositionweb.es

Vergne was second in a first great result for Techeetah, while the podium was completed by Sam Bird for Virgin Racing.

Monaco ePrix

With di Grassi reengaging in the fight for the drivers' championship, the fifth round of the championship was reached in the Principality of Monaco, where Buemi achieved pole followed by di Grassi, resuming the classic fight between the two.

Buemi kept the first position at the start and increased his lead in the opening laps. The Swiss was intractable, regaining his advantage each time the safety car eliminated the differences between drivers, which earned him his fourth victory of the season and continue to impose his reign on the season.

Diariomotor.com

Di Grassi was second, minimizing the loss of points, while Nick Heidfeld again achieved a new podium for Mahindra.

After the last two races, Buemi's lead over di Grassi in the standings was reduced to 14 points, ensuring a new and even season.

For its part, Renault e.Dams had a 37-point advantage over Audi, well above both teams such as Mahindra, Techeetah and Virgin, which once again left the championship at the mercy of the two main teams of the first years of the competition.

Paris ePrix

Paris repeated again in the third season of the championship, and Buemi continued to assert his authority from qualifying, getting pole, with a di Grassi who started 14th and it was difficult to keep closing the gap with his greatest rival.

Buemi started well again and increased his lead over Vergne in the opening laps. Meanwhile, di Grassi was complicating the championship by trying to overtake Félix da Costa on lap 16, hitting both cars. The Brazilian tried to set up the car to seek the fastest lap and score some points, but finally had to retire 11 laps before the end.

Thus, Buemi managed to win his fifth race of the season and gain a significant advantage of 43 points over di Grassi, who was still comfortable in second position. Second was the Argentine José María López for the Virgin team. Heidfeld completed a new podium and together with his teammate Felix Rosenqvist, fourth, achieved a very good result for Mahindra.

Renault e.Dams, meanwhile, achieved a 90-point lead over Audi, which in turn was just 21 points behind Mahindra.

Berlin ePrix 1

This season, Berlin joined the double rounds to celebrate a double race, as did New York and Montreal later to close out the championship.

With just three locations and six races left in the competition, di Grassi took pole position in the first German race with the intention of closing the gap in qualifying with Buemi. The Brazilian made a good start and the Mahindra drivers advanced to second and third to try to catch him. Meanwhile, Buemi was fighting to reach 12th place.

After the pit stop, Rosenqvist managed to overtake di Grassi, who was positioned between the two Mahindra drivers. The race ended like this, with the Brazilian between the two drivers of the Indian team, with the Swede's first victory in the category. Rosenqvist, after several successes in the Macau Grand Prix and the Formula 3 Masters, began to alternate in the 2016 Blancpain GT, Indy Lights, DTM and Formula E.

Sextoanillo.com

Di Grassi's second-place finish, in contrast to Buemi, who had to retire, reduced the point difference between the two to just 22 points.

The gap between Renault e.Dams and Audi narrowed to 56 points, while Mahindra's recent strong results put the Indian team in third place just 14 points behind the German.

Berlin ePrix 2

For the second race in Berlin, Rosenqvist continued his good work in Germany taking pole, while Buemi started second trying to make up for the disaster of the previous race. Di Grassi qualified seventh.

Rosenqvist and Heidfeld got upset at the pit stop, losing valuable time that did not prevent the Swede from continuing in the lead after the mandatory stoppage to change cars. However, after reviewing the images, he suffered a 10-second penalty that ended up relegating him to second place and giving Sébastien Buemi the sixth victory of the season.

Rincondelmotor.com

Behind Buemi and Rosenqvist were the two Audi drivers, di Grassi and Abt. This meant that the points difference between Buemi and di Grassi increased to 32 points and that Rosenqvist rose to third place in the standings.

In terms of teams, the difference between Renault e.Dams and Audi increased slightly to 58 points.

New York ePrix 1

This season, the American test was in New York, also with a double career. Briton Alex Lynn surprised by getting pole with Virgin, while di Grassi was 10th in the standings and Buemi... was unable to participate in the event.

The date of the New York ePrix coincided with the World Endurance Championship test in Germany, where Buemi participated alongside Toyota. The controversy surrounding the FIA for not having respected the calendar of both competitions meant jeopardizing Buemi's great season in Formula E, especially considering that New York was a double date.

Buemi was replaced by Pierre Gasly, who finished seventh just ahead of his Renault e.Dams teammate Nicolas Prost. In all this uproar, Sam Bird achieved his fourth win in the category and his first of the season.

Autobild.es

The two Techeetah drivers, Frenchmen Jean-Éric Vergne and Stéphane Sarrazin completed the podium in a good race for the Chinese team.

Di Grassi was fourth, being able to take better advantage of Buemi's absence to close the gap in qualifying.

New York ePrix 2

For the second race, Sam Bird was taking advantage of his streak to get pole. Di Grassi again had a mediocre classification to start in ninth position.

Bird was again the fastest in New York achieving a second victory and thus closing a more than satisfactory day for the Briton.

Motoresapleno.com.ar

This time those who completed the podium were the Mahindra riders: Rosenqvist and Heidfeld. Fourth was Pierre Gasly in a good debut in the category, and fifth was Lucas di Grassi, who could have made better use of Buemi's absence at the weekend.

Despite the loss of Sébastien Buemi in both races, the Swiss managed to maintain the lead, although now only 20 points clear of di Grassi.

In terms of team standings, the gap between Renault e.Dams and Audi only narrowed by two points, leaving both to 56 points with just two races to go.

Montreal ePrix 1

This third edition of the championship ended in Canada and not in London, once again with a tight finish and with Buemi leading di Grassi by 20 points, repeating the fight of the previous season.

In what was expected of this close fight, di Grassi achieved pole position in the first race while Buemi would come alongside him in the race. The Brazilian managed to maintain his position at the end of the race, achieving a victory with the intention of fighting until the end.

Inmotion.dhl

To the happiness of the Brazilian driver, Buemi was disqualified after the race when he found that his car did not meet the minimum weight of 880 kilos (driver included).

This turned the standings upside down as di Grassi took the championship lead by 18 points ahead of Buemi and was now the favorite to win the title.

Audi was 33 points behind Renault e.Dams and therefore entered the last race with slight chances of also winning the team championship.

Montreal ePrix 2

With everything to resolve came the second race in Canada, and the last of the competition. Felix Rosenqvist achieved pole by showing his good work in the final part of the championship, while di Grassi was 5th in the standings and Buemi complicated the championship in 14th place.

The victory was achieved by Jean-Éric Vergne for Techeetah, a team that was having a great championship final. In the first race in Montreal he had managed to get his two pilots to the podium.

However, the emotion was somewhat further behind. Di Grassi beat Buemi in the final classification. The Brazilian was seventh, while the Swiss finished 11th. This meant that Lucas di Grassi managed to become the Formula E world champion with a 24-point advantage over Buemi; Although there will always be the question of whether the Swiss could have revalidated the title if he had been able to participate in the double appointment in New York.

Montrealquebeclatino.com

The result of Canada did not affect the classification of teams. Renault e.Dams was proclaimed champion for the third time, winning all the Formula E championships held since its inception, with a 20-point advantage over Audi, which once again claimed the runner-up. Behind, Mahindra took third place 33 points behind the Germans.

Conceptcarz.com

FINAL CLASSIFICATION 2016-2017

Lucas di Grassi	181	Renault e.Dams	268
Sébastien Buemi	157	ABT Schaeffler Audi Sport	248
Felix rosenqvist	127	Mahindra Racing	215
Sam bird	122	DS Virgin Racint	190
Jean-Éric Vergne	117	Techeetah	156
Nicolas Prost	93	NextEV NIO	59
Nick heidfeld	88	MS Amlin Andretti	34
Daniel Abt	67	Faraday Future Dragon Racing	33
Jose Maria Lopez	65	Venturi	30
Stéphane Sarrazin	36	Panasonic Jaguar Racing	27
Nelson Piquet Jr.	33		
Oliver Turvey	26		
Robin frijns	24		
Mitch Evans	22		
Loïc Duval	20		
Pierre Gasly	18		
Maro engel	16		
Jérome D'Ambrosio	13		
Tom dillmann	12		
António Felix da Costa	10		
Adam Carroll	5		
Esteban Gutierrez	5		
Alex lynn	3		
Mike conway	0		
Ma Qing Hua	0		

Formulaspy.com

2017-2018: the year of the establishment of the category

The fourth season of Formula E was organized without major changes in its structure, which showed the solidity and confidence in a young competition, but which augured a good future.

The electric power was increased to allow the cars to reach 241 hp in the progressive objective of achieving an ever faster competition.

The aim was therefore to finish off Renault e.Dams, the only team capable of winning the world championship in the first three editions. To maintain its dominance, the French team continued to rely on its regular drivers: Sébastien Buemi and Nicolas Prost. Audi, the main rival and aspiring to compete for the title, also kept Lucas di Grassi and Daniel Abt. It only remained to see if drivers like Sam Bird or Felix Rosenqvist or teams like Techeetah or Mahindra that had finished with good results the previous season, could join the fight for either of the two titles.

Hong Kong ePrix 1

Hong Kong reopened the championship, this time with a double race to begin to unravel the possible unknowns of this new season.

Vergne secured pole for Techeetah in the first race, in a qualifying in which di Grassi was sixth and Buemi ninth, in what could prematurely be seen as a change in the dynamics of previous years.

Following an IndyCar-style traffic jam caused by Lotterer colliding with the barrier while trying to avoid Piquet after a mistake by the Brazilian, the race had to stop and resume half an hour later.

On the fifth lap, Buemi and di Grassi resumed the hostilities of other years clashing, as the Brazilian did not leave enough space for the Swiss. After the pit stop, Buemi's car stopped, and although he was able to restart it, he would no longer have a chance to fight for the race.

Meanwhile, Sam Bird, who had managed to lead the race after overtaking Vergne at the restart, managed to finish first and claim the first victory of the season for DS Virgin Racing.

Michelinracingusa.com

Vergne managed to hold at least second place for a Techeetah team that started the new season as well as the previous one had finished, and third was Nick Heidfeld with Mahindra, also finishing on podium positions as he had frequently done in the second half of the championship. last year.

As for the duel of favorites, di Grassi ended with a lost lap and Buemi finished in 11th place.

Hong Kong ePrix 2

After a somewhat disappointing first race, the favorites continued their poor qualifying performance, finishing at the bottom of the grid. Meanwhile, Rosenqvist took pole for Mahindra.

The race started behind the safety car due to circuit lighting errors. The Swede, who had achieved pole, also took the victory, although for this he had to fight with the Swiss Edoardo Mortara from Venturi, who only lost the first position when his car began to have problems with energy regeneration.

Vehiculoselectricos.co

Mitch Evans took third place to secure an important podium for the Panasonic Jaguar Racing team.

After the first two races, Sam Bird led the drivers' standings and in the Mahindra and Virgin teams they stood out above the rest.

Neither Buemi nor di Grassi were among the top five drivers, and neither were Renault e.Dams nor Audi among the top five teams, which finally allowed us to think about a major change in the category.

Marrakech ePrix

For the third round of the championship, Morocco repeated on the calendar. Buemi took pole, trying to keep his role as the favorite after his poor performance in Hong Kong.

However, he was defeated in his fight with Rosenqvist, who planned a better strategy and came with more energy to the final part of the race to get ahead of the Swiss and take his second victory of the season.

Hibridosyelectricos.com

The podium was completed by Sam Bird, who again gave a good performance to Virgin Racing, although he was not able to maintain the lead that was passed to Felix Rosenqvist.

In terms of teams, Mahindra had the lead in the first position followed by DS Virgin Racing.

Santiago de Chile ePrix

For the fourth round, the world championship moved to Chile where Vergne achieved a new pole, confirming the good start for Techeetah. Buemi was second and di Grassi was third in the standings.

Frenchman Jean-Éric Vergne was able to turn pole into victory, and not only that, but his teammate was second, achieving between them the first double in the history of Formula E, achieved by the Chinese team Techeetah.

Formularapida.net

Buemi accompanied the Techeetah on the podium, regaining some of his glory but without reaching the dominance of previous years.

Vergne's victory put him ahead of the championship, while Techeetah's double put the Chinese team at the top of the standings, 2 points clear of Mahindra.

Mexico City ePrix

The World Championship was held in America for the fifth race, in this case in Mexico City, in one of the most even seasons so far due to the slowdown in performance of Renault e.Dams and Audi.

Rosenqvist achieved pole position for Mahindra in a year that was starting very well for the Indian team. However, the Swede ended up retiring due to a lack of energy in his car.

This allowed Daniel Abt to claim victory in a season in which Audi urgently needed to accumulate points.

Snaplap.net

Second was Oliver Turvey for the NIO team and third Buemi, who seemed to find his good feelings again.

The Mahindra disaster (Heidfeld had to withdraw also due to a hydraulic pump failure) was not taken advantage of by Techeetah as much as they would have liked, as only Vergne was able to score in fifth position, although it would be enough to maintain the lead 9 points per on top of the Indian team.

Vergne, for his part, held the individual lead 12 points above Rosenqvist.

Punta del Este ePrix

This unusual season continued in Uruguay for its sixth round. Di Grassi achieved pole position in an attempt to bring the championship back to the trend of previous years.

However, throughout the race, the present would end up prevailing over the past. Vergne edged out di Grassi in a passionate and exciting battle to confirm himself as the new title contender and to continue to allow Techeetah to dominate the championship.

Rincondelmotor.com

Third was Sam Bird for a good Virgin year that at the beginning of the season seemed like it could be better.

Vergne left Punta del Este even more in the lead, 30 points ahead of Rosenqvist, as did Techeetah, who led Mahindra by 27 points, which in turn began to worry more about keeping second place against Virgin at just 9 points from them.

Rome ePrix

With the debut of an Italian headquarters in Formula E, Rosenqvist once again achieved a new pole in his attempt to continue to stay in the fight for the championship. But once again, the Swede had to retire due to a broken suspension in his car, losing another opportunity to close the gap in points with Vergne in qualifying.

Rosenqvist's withdrawal made it easier for Sam Bird to score his second win of the season and overtake the Swede in the standings, putting himself just 18 points behind Vergne after finishing fifth in Rome.

Onmotor.es

Sam Bird's victory for Virgin did not serve to reduce the gap with Techeetah, on the contrary, it increased to 34 points after third place for André Lotterer and fifth for Vergne for the Chinese team.

Paris ePrix

Entering the final part of the championship, Formula E moved once again to Paris where Vergne took pole followed by Sam Bird. With this it became increasingly clear that the Buemi-di Grassi fight was in the past.

Vergne achieved a new victory in relative comfort, although draining the energy of his car to the maximum.

Diariomotor.com

Di Grassi was second and Sam Bird fought for third place against Lotterer, who finally, after hitting him from behind, managed to overcome to complete the podium. Vergne increased his qualifying lead over Sam Bird to 31 points after the French event. In the same way, Techeetah also managed to get away from Virgin, keeping the first place 55 points behind the British team.

Berlin ePrix

Starting the last third of the season it came to the Germany race. In it, Daniel Abt got pole for an Audi team that could not maintain the level of previous years.

Abt had no problems getting the victory in Berlin, being the fastest on the German circuit followed by his partner di Grassi who was not able to fight, supposedly due to problems in the direction. The double was a great result for Audi, who needed such a win to regain their former glory.

G-store.it

After the two Audi drivers, Jean-Éric Vergne completed the podium, with three races remaining, leading Sam Bird by 40 points (with Felix Rosenqvist third, far behind 76 points behind the leader). This meant that Vergne could already be proclaimed champion in the next round.

As for the teams, Teechetah maintained the lead, but this time the second position was achieved by Audi, who with the double was put to 44 points and again aspired to the championship.

Zurich ePrix

Switzerland made their debut in the Formula E championship with the tenth race of the season, the last one before the final double appointment in New York. Mitch Evans secured an unexpected pole for Panasonic Jaguar Racing which he was unable to properly exploit as he finished seventh in the race.

The victory went to di Grassi, who in the last part of the championship seemed to have regained his champion level.

Autobild.es

Di Grassi's victory saw Audi cut Techeetah 11 points, putting him just 33 behind the Chinese team, behind Lotterer's fourth place and Vergne's tenth.

Sam Bird took advantage of the championship leader's lackluster performance and finished second, cutting Vergne 17 points and moving 23 out of first place. The two championships were even while Jérome d'Ambrosio took third place on the podium for Dragon Racing.

New York ePrix 1

With everything to be decided, the last double race on US soil was reached. Vergne was the favorite to win the drivers' championship with a 23-point advantage, while the fight for the team championship was very close between Techeetah and Audi, with only 11 points of difference.

In the first race, Buemi achieved a somewhat late pole to fight for the championship, and that in fact did not help him to achieve victory, although it did to get on the podium in third position in a season in which he was not achieving his best Results for Renault e.Dams.

The victory went to di Grassi, in a great finale to the season, although this new victory would already be insufficient to contest the drivers' championship. His teammate Daniel Abt finished in second place, in a new double for Audi which in this case was very important for the team championship.

V8project.com.ar

Vergne finished fifth and added 10 more points... which was enough to proclaim himself the Formula E world champion, as Sam Bird, ninth, was 31 points behind the Frenchman. This meant that even if he got the 25 points from the second race plus the extras for pole and fastest lap, he could no longer catch up with the leader.

Motorlat.com

New York ePrix 2

With Frenchman Jean-Éric Vergne already champion of the fourth Formula E drivers' championship, the excitement of the second New York race and the last of the competition focused on the team championship, where Techeetah started with an advantage, although only with a 5-point lead over Audi, which was making a big final part of the competition.

The pole went to Buemi, but the emotion was behind him. Techeetah drivers started second and third, while Audi drivers came fourth and fifth. Vergne also overtook Buemi at the first corner, bringing the Chinese team even closer to the title.

The battle between both teams was intense, Lotterer and Di Grasi got to touch. Then, on lap three, it was announced that there would be an investigation into the two Techeetah drivers for their behavior at the start.

Lotterer was penalized with a pit stop after which he dropped to fifteenth place, putting Techeetah in trouble. In addition, di Grassi overtook Buemi and took second. Meanwhile, Daniel Abt overtook Piquet and placed fifth, improving Audi's positions in the race. Abt also set the fastest lap, which earned additional points.

As di Grassi tried to catch up with Vergne, Daniel Abt took third place, and Audi began to dream of the championship. The Brazilian tried to overtake Vergne, but although the fight was exciting and they even touched, finally the Frenchman got the victory for Techeetah.

With Vergne first and German André Lotterer ninth, they had 27 points. For their part, di Grassi second and Daniel Abt third added 33 points, plus an additional one for the German's fastest lap.

With these figures, Audi was ahead of Techeetah in the standings and won the team championship in the last race by two points. After two consecutive runners-up in the shadow of Renault e.Dams, the German team finally achieved the long-awaited victory and became the champion of the fourth season of Formula E.

Rincondelmotor.com

FINAL CLASSIFICATION 2017-2018

Driver	Points	Team	Points
Jean-Éric Vergne	198	Audi Sport ABT Schaeffler	264
Lucas di Grassi	144	Techeetah	262
Sam bird	143	DS Virgin Racing	160
Sébastien Buemi	125	Mahindra Racing	138
Daniel Abt	120	Renault e.Dams	133
Felix rosenqvist	96	Panasonic Jaguar Racing	119
Mitch Evans	68	Venturi Formula E Team	72
André Lotterer	64	NIO Formula E Team	47
Nelson Piquet Jr.	51	Dragon Racing	41
Oliver Turvey	46	MS&AD Andretti Formula E	24
Nick heidfeld	42		
Maro engel	31		
Edoardo Mortara	29		
Jèrome d'Ambrosio	27		
António Felix da Costa	20		
Alex lynn	17		
Jose Maria Lopez	14		
Tom dillmann	12		
Nicolas Prost	8		
Tom blomqvist	4		
Luca filippi	1		
Stéphane Sarrazin	0		
Ma Qing Hua	0		
Kamui kobayashi	0		
Neel jani	0		

Caranddriver.com

The Gen2: a step ahead in competition

For the fifth season, Formula E decided to take a huge step in its evolution through the design of a new racing car, the Spark STR05e, better known as Gen2.

This new car allowed a higher speed, allowing it to reach 280 km / h, and managed to accelerate from 0 to 100 in just 2.8 seconds. Figures that improved the previous car thanks to its 250 kW of maximum power.

But the highlight of the new car from the show, almost above its new speed, was the fact that the car finally had the ability to pack enough energy to endure a full race, avoiding the strange pit stops to change. of car. This was a necessary change not only for the show, but for the prestige of the competition, since now it could represent the future of the electric automotive with more suitable battery charges.

The new 800-volt battery was developed this time by McLaren, with cells built by Sony and assembled by Lucid Motors.

Motor.es

The Attack Mode: more excitement and overtaking

With a new car with a battery capable of withstanding the entire race ... pit stops were made unnecessary, threatening the strategic content of the races.

To fix it, Attack Mode was developed. These new regulations forced to leave the ideal circuit line in a certain area as many times as the FIA determined before the race.

Leaving the line supposes the loss of a few tenths that, in case of being pursued by a rival, in most cases means losing the position. That is why it is essential that the drivers choose the right moment to do this compulsory step on the less usual line to try not to lose position.

Formulaeweb.es

However, when passing through the Attack Mode zone, the pilot receives an extra 25 kW of power that can be used to recover the possible position lost due to necessarily leaving the ideal line.

How does this affect your career? In more overtaking. The step to activate Attack Mode means that many drivers lose a position ... but in return they receive the opportunity to regain it with the extra power, if they are able to use it correctly to achieve overtaking and regain position.

Autopista.es

2018-2019: the championship is revolutionized

The fifth season of the competition revolutionized the championship, and not only because of the inclusion of a new car, but because of its consequences.

The fact that the main weakness of the vehicles, the fragility of their batteries, was eliminated, attracted new interested teams. An electric car with energy capable of withstanding a first-rate race is a good claim for brands to show the efficiency of electric vehicles.

One of the most powerful brands to join the competition this season was BMW, in collaboration with the Andretti team structure.

Diariomotor.com

Nissan also joined the competition through the e.Dams structure that Renault was leaving. The most successful team in the competition thus opened a new stage seeking to regain its dominance through the Japanese brand.

Mercedes also wanted to "test" the competition, and did so covertly through the new HWA Racelab team. The objective was to get to know the competition to be able to access it as a Mercedes with greater preparation, to try to maintain the fame and authority that it was already achieving in Formula 1.

Artsation.com

Another important change was the establishment of the 45-minute races. The duration of the races would no longer be for a certain number of laps, but would end when 45 minutes passed from the start, a final lap was completed. This made it possible not to lengthen the races so much, especially considering the large number of incidents and security cars that tended to appear.

In turn, the new regulations also included the obligation to include the halo, a safety measure that Formula 1 had already implemented and which had been taken into account when designing the Gen2.

One of the characteristics of the halo is that it lit up so that you could tell when the pilot activated the extra power of Attack Mode or Fanboost.

Fiaformulae.com

With all these novelties, a championship was looming with many unknowns and without knowing exactly where each team would end up relocating, without counting the new ones who participated for the first time.

Al-Diriyah ePrix

To continue the novelties this season, the championship started in a new place: Saudi Arabia. Portuguese António Félix da Costa took pole position for a BMW i Andretti team that started with a bang.

The Portuguese rider managed to maintain the first position on the last lap, and after a tough fight with Vergne, he achieved the first victory of the season. BMW opened with victory in the competition.

Motor.es

Reigning champion Jean-Éric Vergne started with a second place while Jérome d'Ambrosio took the last place on the podium for Mahindra.

The change from e.Dams to Nissan resulted in a sixth place for Buemi and a seventh for Oliver Rowland of Britain who replaced Nicolas Prost on the team.

Reigning team champion Audi finished with Abt in eighth place and di Grassi in ninth.

Marrakech ePrix

Morocco once again hosted a Formula E event, in this case the second of this renewed season, where British Sam Bird achieved pole position for Virgin.

Shortly after starting the race, Vergne collided with Bird, so that a part of the Frenchman's Techeetah was lodged in the Briton's car, complicating the race, although he was finally able to finish third. Second was his teammate Robin Frijns in a good race for Virgin who got both drivers to finish on the podium.

Meanwhile, the victory went to Jérome d'Ambrosio, in a Mahindra team that ended up reaping good results the previous season.

Motor.es

The victory of the Belgian from Mahindra allowed him to lead the standings with a 12-point advantage over Antonio Félix da Costa and Jean-Éric Vergne.

As for the teams, the consistency of the Techeetahs allowed them to lead the Chinese team with 7 points of advantage over Mahindra and BMW-Andretti.

Santiago ePrix

The season continued with a third race in Santiago de Chile, where qualifying brought some nostalgia with di Grassi's pole position for Audi and Buemi's second place for Nissan e.Dams. However, the race would end in a totally different way, oblivious to the great rivalry of both drivers. The Swiss had to retire due to a broken suspension and the Brazilian finished 13th.

Meanwhile, Sam Bird continued to put on great performances, clinching victory in the Chile race for Virgin Racing.

Thebestf1.es

German Pascal Wehrlein secured second place to continue Mahindra's strong start to the season, while Daniel Abt completed the podium for an Audi team that refused to give up the fight for a championship that had changed a lot since their victory.

Sam Bird was the leader of the classification two points above Félix da Costa, both well above the rest of the drivers.

For its part, Virgin Racing took the top spot in the team standings.

Mexico City ePrix

In Mexico the first third of the championship was completed with the pole of Pascal Wehrlein confirming the rise of Mahindra, followed by di Grassi.

Five minutes later, a strong accident by Piquet hitting Vergne's Techeetah from behind and then Alexander Sims's BMW forced the red flag to be raised.

In the final part of the race, Wehrlein withstood di Grassi's attacks... until he ran out of energy, losing the race at the last corner where the Brazilian managed to overtake him to claim victory.

Elsiglodetorreon.com.mx

The podium in Mexico was completed by Felipe Massa. The former Ferrari driver had joined the Venturi team in this edition of the championship.

Hong Kong ePrix

Hong Kong joined the schedule this season, though not to open it, but as the fifth round on the schedule. In it, Belgian Stoffel Vandoorne gave the surprise by getting pole for HWA, the Mercedes test team.

A new multiple incident between Felipe Nasr and the two Mahindra pilots forced to show the red flag.

With just under 20 minutes to go, Vandoorne had to withdraw due to broadcast problems ending HWA's hopes for victory.

In the closing bars, Sam Bird and Lotterer dominated the race, but the Briton hit the German and both saw their chances of victory vanished.

That allowed the Swiss Edoardo Mortara to get the victory for the Venturi team.

Thechekerredflag.co.uk

Second was di Grassi, who together with Daniel Abt's fourth place achieved a good result for Audi. Third placed in Hong Kong was Robin Frijns for Virgin.

Sanya ePrix

For the sixth round of the season, the championship moved to Sanya, China. In it, Oliver Rowland took pole for Nissan, which was not quite achieving the performance necessary to return e.Dams to its best times.

Rowland could not resist the attack of Vergne, who overtook him in the race to steal the first place that the Frenchman held to achieve victory in China and give Techeetah another victory in his own land.

Autobild.es

Oliver Rowland finished second giving Nissan the first major win of the season. Third was António Félix da Costa for a BMW that had started the season very strong but was struggling to keep up.

With almost half of the season passed, the Portuguese Félix da Costa was leader with a point of advantage over Jérome d'Ambrosio. Not far behind in points were Vergne, Sam Bird and Lucas di Grassi in one of the most even seasons of the competition.

As for the teams, the equality was even greater. Virgin, Mahindra, Audi and Techeetah were separated by just two points, and not far behind them BMW was in fifth place.

Rome ePrix

With great equality in the classification, the Italian event was reached, to see who was able to stand out in both the drivers 'and the teams' titles. Techeetah sought his candidacy to achieve it with the pole of German André Lotterer.

Again and in an exciting race, Lotterer tried to get the victory until on the last lap he was overtaken by New Zealander Mitch Evans who gave Jaguar the first victory.

Ahoraroma.com

Third was Stoffel Vandoorne for HWA, so the main protagonists of the season left Rome without good results. This caused the classification to change abruptly again and now Jérome d'Ambrosio, Félix da Costa, Lotterer and Mitch Evans were leading the table with only 4 points difference between them.

Techeetah stood out slightly in the team rankings, but with Virgin, Mahindra and Audi close behind. BMW was lowered slightly.

Paris ePrix

In the eighth race of the championship, in France, it was the right time for a driver to strike a stroke of authority and begin to excel in pursuit of the championship. Pascal Wehrlein took pole for Mahindra, followed by the two Nissan drivers, Rowland and Buemi, in qualifying.

The race started behind the safety car and became one of the most chaotic races of the entire competition with the onset of rain. Only when the rain stopped did the drivers seem to gain some control and compete effectively.

The driver who best adapted to the changing weather conditions was Dutch Robin Frijns, who thus achieved victory for Virgin Racing.

Express.co.uk

André Lotterer took second place to give Techeetah a good score, followed by the two Audi drivers: Daniel Abt and di Grassi.

The French rain allowed Frijns and Lotterer, both separated by a single point, to separate slightly from the rest in qualifying.

Techeetah also got some advantage in the team championship, although everything was still really level.

Monaco ePrix

In Monaco the last third of the championship began, where with such equality, each victory began to have even more importance. Rowland got the pole for a Nissan that achieved good classifications that later did not materialize in good results in the race.

This time Rowland failed to turn pole into victory, but at least it served him to finish second. The victory went to Vergne, who did not give up and maintained his options to revalidate the title, and gave Techeetah a little more advantage.

Motor.es

Third was Felipe Massa, who returned to get a new podium for Venturi.

After the test of the Principality, Vergne took the leadership of the championship, although only with a point of advantage over Lotterer and six over Frijns. Félix da Costa and di Grassi stayed close to them.

As for the team championship, the equality was broken there and Techeetah got 38 points ahead of Virgin.

Berlin ePrix

Berlin remained on the Formula E calendar to continue this exciting end to the season. Buemi got the pole remembering old times, although he no longer had great options to fight for the championship.

Germany served to remember the constant fights in the past between Buemi and di Grassi, where this time the Brazilian was victorious.

Gacetadelmotor.com

Third was Vergne who maintained the lead, but found a new competitor in di Grassi, second in the standings just 6 points behind the French.

In the team standings, Techeetah also held the top spot, but Audi was close to 25 points.

Bern ePrix

With only three races to play, the World Cup traveled to Switzerland but in this case to the city of Bern. Vergne got pole, in a clear intention to settle his first place in the championship.

The Frenchman managed to maintain the first position at the end of the race and achieved a victory that, if not definitive, at least served him to get closer to a new world title.

Graining.es

Second was Mitch Evans who returned to achieve one of the sporadic successes of Panasonic Jaguar. Buemi managed to get back on the podium in third place in a Nissan e.Dams that seemed to improve his performance in the final part of the championship.

New York ePrix 1

With Vergne leading the drivers' championship with 32 points of advantage and Techeetah well above the rival teams, the double appointment of New York was reached, a city that once again closed the championship.

For the first race, Buemi took pole, showing the improvement of Nissan e.Dams in the final part of the championship. In fact, the Swiss managed to achieve victory.

Thebestf1.es

Mitch Evans was second, with Panasonic Jaguar being another of the teams that improved in the final part of the competition. The podium was completed by Félix da Costa, who together with his teammate Alexander Sims in fourth position, achieved a good result for a BMW that had achieved good but irregular results throughout the season.

Meanwhile, Jean-Éric Vergne only managed to finish in 15th position and the championship was slightly complicated. With 130 points, he was chased in the standings by di Grassi with 108 points and Mitch Evans with 105, both still with options. In addition, with Buemi's recent victory, the Swiss accumulated 104 points and was faced with an unexpected option to fight for the championship in the last race.

New York ePrix 2

After having lost Vergne part of his great advantage in the first race in which he could have sentenced the championship, he was still the favorite to revalidate the title in the last race of the season. However, a new bad performance like the previous one would give di Grassi, Mitch Evans and Sébastien Buemi the opportunity to clinch the title if they achieved a great result.

While pole position went to Alexander Sims' BMW, Vergne finished 12th in the standings behind his pursuers: Buemi was 3rd, Evans was 8th and di Grassi 11th.

The race was won by Dutch Robin Frijns for Virgin. However, the emotion was further behind.

Vergne finished seventh in the standings adding only 6 points... which would be enough to re-proclaim himself world champion. Di Grassi had crashed, losing all options to win the championship, Mitch Evans finished 17th and Sébastien Buemi achieved a third place that confirmed his good end to the season, and although it was insufficient to snatch the title from Vergne, he managed to finish runner-up.

Kurier.art

While Vergne achieved his second world title in Formula E, his Techeetah team also managed to win a team championship in which they had already managed to distance themselves from the rest in the last part of the championship.

Formularapida.net

FINAL CLASSIFICATION 2018-2019

Jean-Éric Vergne	136	DS Techeetah	222
Sébastien Buemi	119	Audi ABT Schaeffler Team	203
Lucas di Grassi	108	Envision Virgin Racing	191
Robin frijns	106	Nissan e.Dams	190
Mitch Evans	105	BMW i Andretti Motorsport	156
António Felix da Costa	99	Mahindra Racing	125
Daniel Abt	95	Panasonic Jaguar Racing	116
André Lotterer	86	Venturi Formula E Team	88
Sam bird	85	HWA Racelab	44
Oliver Rowland	71	GEOX Dragon	23
Jérome d'Ambrosio	67	NIO Formula E Team	7
Pascal Wehrlein	58		
Alexander sims	57		
Edoardo Mortara	52		
Felipe Massa	36		
Stoffel vandoorne	35		
Maximilian Günther	20		
Alex lynn	10		
Gary Paffett	9		
Oliver Turvey	7		
Jose Maria Lopez	3		
Nelson Piquet Jr.	1		
Tom dillmann	0		
Philip Nasr	0		
Felix rosenqvist	0		

Evpro.es

2019-2020: The arrival of Mercedes... and Porsche

For the sixth season, second since Gen2, the main novelty was the arrival of Mercedes to the championship. Following their undeniable success and absolute dominance in Formula 1, there was a lot of interest to see if the German team would be able to replicate their success in electric competition.

The previous campaign had already used the HWA Racelab team as a test team, but this time it was presented with its name and main structure: Mercedes-Benz EQ Formula E Team. Its squad included the pilots Stoffel Vandoorne and Nyck de Vries. Vandoorne was known for his time in Formula 1 with the McLaren team and de Vries was the reigning Formula 2 champion.

Nj-design.dk

Mercedes was not the only team to join this Formula E season. Another historical and prestigious brand was encouraged to participate: Porsche, with the TAG Heuer Porsche Formula E Team and the drivers Neel Jani and André Lotterer.

These two new entrants increased the prestige and the spectacle of a competition that did not stop growing. However, this would be a difficult season that would be suddenly affected by the coronavirus pandemic.

Diriyah ePrix 1

The championship started again in Saudi Arabia, this time with a double date, with the interest of seeing how the new teams would develop, especially Mercedes.

And the pole was obtained by Alexander Sims for BMW i Andretti that once again started the season strong. Second and third were Stoffel Vandoorne and Nyck de Vries for a Mercedes team that was excited from the first classification.

However, victory would not be for either of them. The first victory of the season was for Sam Bird with a Virgin Racing team that continued to reap good results, and that this season aimed to maintain a better consistency to fight for the titles.

Motoryracing.com

Mercedes did not fare as well as in qualifying, although at least Belgian Stoffel Vandoorne managed to finish third, with the Mercedes team debuting with a podium in Formula E. His teammate De Vryes finished sixth.

Porsche also had a good debut as André Lotterer secured second place for the new championship team.

The new ones were competitive, which augured a different championship than previously seen.

Diriyah ePrix 2

For the second race in the opening double round of the championship, Alexander Sims once again achieved pole position for BMW, while behind him, at least in qualifying, the classic fight between Buemi and di Grassi was resumed.

The Swiss ended up out of the fight for victory after being penalized with ten seconds for an unsafe return to the track. Sims did manage to take advantage of the pole this time to get the victory and become the first leader after the first double test.

Motor.es

Second was di Grassi who maintained his good pace shown in qualifying and third was Vandoorne again to give Mercedes a second podium in his second race in the competition. His teammate, Nyck de Vries, finished 16th after a penalty for overtaking under a yellow flag and a five-second penalty for technical infraction.

Santiago ePrix

After the first double race, he returned to the Chilean classic in Santiago to continue with the third round of the competition, where Mitch Evans was once again at the top of a classification by taking pole for Panasonic Jaguar.

The race, however, was won by BMW, with another great start to the season, but it would not be Sims the winner, but his teammate Maximilian Günther in a passionate fight on the last lap with Felix da Costa. The German became the youngest driver to win a Formula E race.

Racing5.cl

Portuguese António Félix da Costa was second for DS Techeetah at a start to the season that seemed not to be at the level of a team that was the reigning champions.

The podium was completed by Mitch Evans, in that attempt by Panasonic Jaguar to turn sporadic hits into more regularity. Podium which Nyck de Vries had previously held with third place for Mercedes, but which was annulled by a violation of the minimum battery coolant temperature.

Mexico City ePrix

Mexico also repeated once more on the calendar to become the venue for the fourth race of the season, where André Lotterer got pole for a Porsche team that did not start badly in its first season in Formula E, but was still looking for its place. .

Lotterer did not have a great start to the race, losing several positions and not getting a pace commensurate with his classification, and finally ended up retiring after a hit with the barriers.

This was taken advantage of by Mitch Evans, who this time achieved victory and made Panasonic Jaguar one of the best teams in the first third of the championship.

Autox.com

Second was António Félix da Costa, who once again put a Techeetah at the same level as the previous season. Third for his part was Sébastien Buemi, although e.Dams was not in his best years, he was still getting some good results.

After these first four races, Mitch Evans was the leader with just one point ahead of Alexander Sims. A little further away, and also a point away from each other, were António Félix da Costa and Stoffel Vandoorne. The first driver to win a Formula E championship in the standings was di Grassi in fifth position.

In terms of teams, BMW i Andretti led the standings with a 14-point advantage. It was necessary to see if this season he was able to maintain the good start and not lose performance as in the previous one. Behind, Jaguar, Mercedes and Techeetah were second, third and fourth with only two points of difference between them.

And then, the coronavirus broke in.

The pandemic paralyzed the world, and as in other sports, Formula E had to stop and the calendar was canceled. The option that was finally decided to resume it was exceptional and striking: six races in Berlin in just 8 days with the aim of limiting mobility and the possibility of spreading the virus.

Berlin ePrix 1

On August 5 the championship resumed with the first of six races in Berlin. The interest was put in seeing how the stoppage had affected the drivers and teams and if the championship would follow the trend of its beginning or the state of form would have changed enough to revolutionize it.

During this break time, many of the pilots participated in virtual races and competitions, both as individual training and to provide entertainment during the various quarantines.

Formula E organized its own virtual championship with its real drivers for charity purposes. Curious was the case of Daniel Abt, who was accused of cheating since it was not he who participated in the virtual competition, but a professional pilot of this type of competition whom he had hired to impersonate him behind the computer.

Audi expelled him from the team for not fulfilling his virtual commitment, a fact that was attacked by the rest of the drivers, since they considered it an excessive measure and that virtuality should not affect his professional career in that way. The German René Rest replaced Abt at Audi, although he was able to continue in the competition after his signing for the NIO 333 FE team that was released from the Chinese Ma Qing Hua.

Back in the competition, DS Techeetah proved to be the team that recovered the best from the break with the pole position of António Félix da Costa and the second place of Jean-Éric Vergne in qualifying. The Portuguese managed to finish the race with victory, although the French, with problems, finished in the final part of the classification.

Independent.co.uk

Second was André Lotterer in a new good result for Porsche and third Sam Bird returned to get a podium for Virgin.

The Mercedes, with de Vries fourth and Vandoorne sixth, continued to score important points, although without achieving the dominance that everyone expected with their irruption in Formula E.

After the first race in Berlin, Félix da Costa stood out over Evans with a 31-point lead and Techeetah overtook BMW in the team standings.

Berlin ePrix 2

The second race in Berlin was done on the same layout as the first, which allowed Félix da Costa to show his talent on the first circuit deployed over Tempelhof airport to achieve a new pole.

Also this time the Portuguese took the victory, in a very favorable beginning of the restart for him.

Diariomotor.com

Second was Sébastien Buemi, showing his good performance although far from the regularity that made him champion, and third was di Grassi. The Brazilian placed second in the championship standings, in absolute equality with Stoffel Vandoorne and Mitch Evans, although da Costa was away with 68 points of advantage.

Similarly, Techeetah was 65 points ahead of BMW, Nissan e. Dams and Mercedes, the three closely even with each other.

Berlin ePrix 3

For the third race on German soil the layout was changed to create a different circuit. In fact, the organization was based on three double races on three different tracks.

The third classification was dominated by DS Techeetah, but this time by its French driver, Vergne, who finally finished third in the race. His Portuguese teammate finished fourth, thus ending his chances of getting a full win in the frenzied restart in Germany.

The victory went to Max Günther, the young man repeated his triumph with BMW to try to keep the hopes of the German team.

Historiadeportiva.com

Robin Frijns was second with Virgin in a championship that was beginning to point to da Costa and Techeetah as future champions.

Berlin ePrix 4

In the fourth of the six Berlin races to complete the championship, the Techeetah remained intractable: pole for Vergne and second place on the starting grid for Félix da Costa.

The dominance in qualifying moved into the race to get a double that practically sentenced the championship with two races to go. It was enough for the Portuguese to be second to secure the drivers' championship mathematically and thus become Formula E champion for the first time.

Movilidadelectrica.com

Sébastien Buemi accompanied the Techeetah on the podium in a year in which, although he did not dominate as in other seasons, the e.Dams team seemed to regain good feelings.

Berlin ePrix 5

For the fifth test in Germany and the penultimate of the season, the circuit layout was again changed for the last time in a titanic job to build three circuits in just over a week.

Used to seeing very exciting finishes in Formula E, António Félix da Costa's triumph took away some of the excitement from the last two races, although many drivers such as Vandoorne, Vergne, Buemi, Oliver Rowland and Lucas di Grassi still aspired to runner-up.

It was precisely the British Nissan e.Dams, Oliver Rowland, who achieved pole this time and who also managed to transform it into victory to give a leap in quality to his team.

Motor.es

Second was Robin Frijns to score more important points for Virgin while the podium was completed by René Rast, the replacement for Daniel Abt at Audi.

Berlin ePrix 6

With little to define beyond the drivers' runner-up, what would be the last race of the season began at the exceptional restart in Berlin.

Vandoorne got the pole to try to improve the result for Mercedes in his first (official) participation in the category. As in so many times at the restart, the poleman became the winner of the race and the German team thus achieved their first victory in Formula E. And not only that, but Nyck de Vries' second place ended the race. season with a double that saw the team finish in third place in the standings. In addition, Belgian Stoffel Vandoorne managed to finish runner-up in the world championship.

Automundo.com.ar

Sébastien Buemi managed to get on the podium behind the Mercedes to confirm the good end of the season for Nissan e.Dams, who with this result managed to finish second in the team standings.

Meanwhile, the Chinese team DS Techeetah held a team championship that they had already secured long before. With two world titles achieved, it was just one more championship than those achieved by Renault e.Dams, the team with the most wins in the category.

Noticias.autocosmos.com.co

FINAL CLASSIFICATION 2019-2020

Driver	Points	Team	Points
António Felix da Costa	158	DS Techeetah	244
Stoffel vandoorne	87	Nissan e.Dams	167
Jean-Éric Vergne	86	Mercedes-Benz EQ Formula E	147
Sébastien Buemi	84	Envision Virgin Racing	121
Oliver Rowland	83	BMW i Andretti Motorsport	118
Lucas di Grassi	77	Audi Sport ABT Schaeffler	114
Mitch Evans	71	Panasonic Jaguar Racing	81
André Lotterer	71	TAG Heuer Porsche	79
Maximilian Günther	69	Mahindra Racing	49
Sam bird	63	ROKiT Venturi Racing	44
Nyck de vries	60	GEOX Dragon	two
Robin frijns	58	NIO 333 FAITH	0
Alexander sims	49		
Edoardo Mortara	41		
René Rast	29		
Jérome d'Ambrosio	19		
Alex lynn	16		
Pascal Wehrlein	14		
James Calado	10		
Neel jani	8		
Daniel Abt	8		
Felipe Massa	3		
Brandon hartley	2		
Oliver Turvey	0		
Nico Müller	0		
Tom blomqvist	0		
Sergio Sette Camara	0		
Ma Qing Hua	0		

Fast-mag.com

2021: The World Championship

In 2021, the competition's seventh season, the championship officially became the FIA World Championship, joining Formula 1, WRC, WEC and the World Rallycross Championship in this category. With this new category, the competition aspired to gain recognition and to establish itself among the main automobile competitions in the world.

For this seventh season of Formula E there were no major technical changes. In fact, the goal was simply to be able to adhere to the calendar without incidents or cancellations, after a year in which the pandemic put all sports in difficulties.

The next revolution in competition will come with the Gen3, the new car that is more powerful (350 kW maximum), light and fast. The most characteristic of this new vehicle will be its ability to be recharged in the race, which will add the classic pit-stop to the competition.

To do this, the FIA will force the development of a car capable of feeding itself energetically with fast charges of a maximum of 30 seconds. Once again, Formula E has to be shown as a showcase for the electric future, and charging time is one of the problems that most affects the sale of electric vehicles. However, the arrival of the Gen3 is planned for the 2022-2023 season.

Yes, a new version of the Gen2 called Gen2 EVO was planned which, due to economic difficulties after the pandemic, was suspended. Therefore, and with the same benefits, a season similar to the previous one was expected.

As for the most prominent driver changes, Sam Bird left Virgin to join Jaguar replacing James Calado. Nick Cassidy replaced Bird at Virgin.

The legendary Ferrari driver Felipe Massa finally left the competition. This was replaced in Venturi by Norman Nato. In Venturi, they also signed Jérome d'Ambrosio as deputy director.

René Rast was confirmed as a driver for Audi, having replaced in the last part of the previous season the sanctioned Daniel Abt.

Wehrlein signed for Porsche, replacing Neel Jani, with the aim of improving the team's performance in the competition.

Alexander Sims left BMW, being replaced by Jake Dennis. Sergio Sette Camara joined Dragon after having participated in the team in the final races of 2020 and Tom Blomqvist replaced Ma Qinghua at NIO 333.

Diriyah ePrix 1

The World Championship began in Saudi Arabia with a double race, with the particularity of being the first night race of the competition.

In it, the Dutch Nyck de Vries achieved pole in a sign that Mercedes had not reached the championship to settle for the third position of teams, while Pascal Wehrlein achieved the second position on the starting grid for Porsche, team of which better performance had been expected the previous season after joining the championship.

Nyck de Vries took advantage of the first position on the starting grid and made a good start to begin to gain an advantage over his pursuers.

From behind, René Rast attacked Wehrlein's Porsche with his Audi to overtake him, get second position and chase Nyck. Meanwhile, Mortara was squeezing the power of his Venturi to overtake Wehrlein and take third place.

After two safety cars caused by the collision between Bird and Lynn, and Günther's accident, there were five minutes remaining, which Nyck took advantage of to drive away again in a brilliant race for the Dutchman.

Behind him, Mortara managed to overtake Rast to take second position, while Evans with his Jaguar also overtook Rast, this time snatching third position from him.

After the checkered flag, Nyck achieved his first victory in Formula E, accompanied by Mortara and Evans on the podium.

Revistasafetycar.com

The current champion team drivers, DS Techeetah, Félix Da Costa and Jean Éric-Vergne, were 11th and 15th in a difficult start for the Chinese team.

Diriyah ePrix 2

In Diriyah's second race, Robin Frijns claimed pole for Virgin, while Nyck was unable to qualify due to a suspension for Mercedes after several incidents in the third practice session.

Frijns managed to defend the first position at the start of the race against Sette Camara, who had to try to defend himself from Sam Bird, who did manage to snatch second position from him.

Throughout the race, the DS Techeetah riders made a great comeback that allowed Vergne to reach third position, albeit far behind the two leaders.

On lap 24, Sam Bird was battling Robin Frijns, and after having swapped positions several times in a magnificent fight, the Jaguar driver managed to overtake him to take first position again. Shortly afterwards, Günther and Evans suffered an accident that forced them to show the red flag, thus ending the race with victory for Bird.

Carmania.mx

Dutchman Robin Frijns had to settle for second place for Virgin, while Da Costa completed the podium for DS Techeetah's consolation.

The Dragon-Penske drivers, the Brazilian Sette Camara and the Swiss Nico Müller, finished in fifth and sixth position in a very good unexpected result for the North American team.

Rome ePrix 1

The second event of the season was in Rome, also with a double career. In the first one, Belgian Stoffel Vandoorne got pole for a Mercedes team that was thus recovering from the penalty in Diriyah's second race.

The race started behind the safety car due to the rain, which retired after five minutes. Vandoorne tried to defend himself against Lotterer's Porsche, and the two touched when the Belgian tried to block his way. This allowed Oliver Rowland to reach the top position with his Nissan.

Rowland was penalized for exceeding the 200 kW limit, allowing Di Grassi to take first place. Behind, he was chased by the Techeetah driver, Vergne, and in third position Robin Frijns with the Virgin.

Vergne risked being the first to activate the attack mode, but he got the strategy right since later, when di Grassi had to pass through the activation zone, he was able to overcome him to obtain the first position.

Vergne was once again the first to activate the attack mode for the second time, losing positions, but later regaining first place with the extra power achieved. De Vries and di Grassi touched each other, helping Vergne to gain more of an advantage as the leader.

Despite the incident, di Grassi managed to come back to threaten Vergne, overtaking him on lap 20, but a technical problem caused him to lose first position.

Vergne regained first place, and a touch between the two Mercedes forced the safety car to be brought out which ended the race, with victory for the Frenchman and with DS Techeetah getting a win again.

Viajesycarreras.com

The two Jaguar drivers completed the podium, with Briton Sam Bird in second place and New Zealander Mitch Evans in third.

Rome ePrix 2

For the second round in Rome, Nick Cassidy took pole for Virgin, followed by Frenchman's Norman Nato's Venturi and Pascal Wehrlein's Porsche.

Again, the race started behind the safety car, as there were still some wet areas on the circuit. When the Safety Car was retired, leader Nick Cassidy locked the rear wheels due to a software glitch turning his car and losing the lead which was held by Norman Nato.

The Frenchman was chased by an aggressive Pascal Wehrlein who tried to steal the first position from him. The German managed to overtake him on lap 3, and shortly afterwards Vandoorne also managed to overtake Nato.

Wehrlein was the last of the drivers at the head of the race to activate attack mode in a failed strategy that saw the Porsche driver lose the top position, now held by Vandoorne.

With half an hour to go, Di Grassi and Buemi collided, once again reliving their eternal rivalry in the competition.

On resuming the race, Alexander Sims overtook Wehrlein to snatch second place from him, while Vandoorne continued to lead away.

On lap 17, Nato overtook Wehrlein to temporarily regain a place on the podium.

A Rene Rast accident with the Audi led to the departure of a safety car that caused Vandoorne to lose all his lead as a leader. However, the Belgian used the fanboost extra power to secure first place and clinch a very important victory for Mercedes following the disqualification at Diriyah and the disaster of the first race in Rome.

Diariomotor.com

Alexander Sims managed to finish in second place giving a good result to Mahindra while Wehrlein managed to complete the podium for Porsche after disqualifying Nato for improper use of energy.

After two events and four races, Briton Sam Bird led the championship with 43 points, above Mitch Evans' 39 points, Robin Frijns' 34, Vandoorne's 33 and Nyck de Vries' 32 in a very tight start. championship.

In terms of teams, Jaguar stood out with 82 points, while Mercedes, despite difficulties, was second with 65 points ahead of defending champion DS Techeetah, who was third with 46.

Valencia ePrix 1

The third double event was held in Valencia, with the novelty that for the first time Formula E was moving to a permanent circuit, instead of being held in the streets of a city adapted for the race.

The double race was held at the Ricardo Tormo circuit, in this challenge that was trying to run on fixed circuits. While the circuits designed specifically for Formula E had strong braking lines to promote energy regeneration, this test was a great challenge for the competition, and at the same time it could be the beginning of the transition to the great and classic circuits.

The pole in the first race went to the Portuguese Da Costa, who seemed to confirm Techeetah's improvement. Mercedes continued their troubles with a five-place grid penalty for Nyck de Vries for causing a collision in Rome, and the disqualification of Vandoorne for a tire infringement.

In rainy conditions, the race started behind the safety car, which once retired, Da Costa took the opportunity to gain an advantage over Günther and Lynn's BMW.

The Safety Car returned again after a collision between Buemi's Nissan, far from its best times, and Lotterer's Porsche. With the restart, Da Costa regained the advantage leading the race.

In the fight for second place, Lynn broke his car while trying to overtake Günther, a fact that Nyck de Vries took advantage of to occupy third position, and a little later he overtook Günther to take second. Shortly after, it was Lynn who overtook Günther to return to podium position.

On the tenth lap, Günther went off the track due to the wet conditions of the asphalt causing the departure of a new safety car. This reappeared later after an accident between Sergio Sette Camara's Dragon and Mitch Evans's Jaguar.

Da Costa did not lose the first position in the resumes, although de Vries was chasing him maintaining a greater amount of energy. With a collision between Mortara and Lotterer, a new safety car appeared and retired with only two laps to go in a hectic race.

And then, chaos happened. Due to the amount of energy to reduce for each appearance of the safety car according to the regulations, many of the drivers were left without energy in the car, including the leader Da Costa, along with Oliver Rowland, Alexander Sims, Alex Lynn and Sam Bird.

These unexpected retirements allowed the Dutch Nyck de Vries to clinch an unexpected victory for Mercedes, despite his initial penalty of five places.

Fast-mag.com

The chaos in Valencia also allowed Stoffel Vandoorne to finish in third place, managing to take two Mercedes cars to the podium despite the Belgian having his qualifying time canceled.

Among them, the Swiss Nico Müller achieved a magnificent position for a Dragon - Penske team not very used to high positions throughout its history.

Valencia ePrix 2

For the second race at Valencia, Jake Dennis took pole with the BMW Andretti, followed by Lotterer's Porsche (who received a three-place penalty for causing an accident in the first race) and Lynn's Mahindra.

Dennis made a good start, defending the first position against Lynn, in a more cautious race trying to reserve energy in the face of the disaster of the first test.

Both drivers moved away from the peloton, while Nato took third place, fighting with Lotterer and Vergne.

Dennis was the first to activate the attack mode, in a successful strategy that allowed him to maintain the first position, while remaining cautious with energy expenditure.

From behind, Nato attacked Lynn, both drivers touched and the Mahindra driver went off the track, while the Frenchman stole second position.

In the first position, Jake Dennis was ordered to slow down the race to avoid additional laps and correctly managed the energy to be able to complete the test and finish in first place, achieving his first victory in the season in which he debuted in the competition and give the victory to BMW.

Racing5.cl

André Lotterer, who managed to overtake Lynn, took second place for Porsche, while the Briton finished third, allowing a good podium for Mahindra.

After the Valencia event, the two Mercedes drivers led the championship, with Nyck de Vries accumulating 57 points and Vandoorne 48, ahead of Sam Bird, Robin Frijns and Mitch Evans.

Mercedes took advantage of the Valencian test, getting the constructors' lead with 23 points of advantage over Jaguar. Audi overtook Techeetah for third place.

Monaco ePrix

In the Principality of Monaco test, Da Costa achieved pole position with the aim of improving his results and being able to fight this season and stay as champion in a problematic classification for Mercedes, with Vandoorne in position 15 as the best classified.

Da Costa held the top position at the start, with Frijns fending off Evans' attack to retain second place.

On the third lap, Frijns managed to overtake Da Costa to put his Virgin in first position. When activating attack mode, he lost the lead, but regained it on lap 13.

Da Costa chased Frijns very closely, closing the gap, while Evans remained in third place. An accident involving Rene Rast with the Audi forced to get out of the safety car and reduce all the distances with 6 minutes remaining.

At the restart, Evans managed to lead the race ahead of Da Costa and Frijns. Evans was told that he had very little energy and tried to defend the position despite the difficulty, but in a brilliant overtake, Da Costa managed to pass him to take victory at the legendary Monaco circuit and bring the Techeetah back to the victory.

Formularapida.net

The low energy of Evans' car also allowed Frijns to overtake him, with the Dutchman finishing second with the Virgin, and relegating the New Zealander to third with his Jaguar.

With this result, Frijns took the world championship lead ahead of Nyck de Vries and Evans, while Mercedes maintained the manufacturers' lead, albeit only two points ahead of Jaguar.

Puebla ePrix 1

Because the Autódromo Hermanos Rodríguez, the usual place for the Mexican test, was busy as a hospital for COVID-19 patients, the Mexico ePrix had to be held at the Autódromo Miguel E. Abed de Amozoc, in Puebla.

For the first race, German Pascal Wehrlein took pole for a Porsche that, although it was in the high positions frequently, failed to materialize its performance in better positions.

Wehrlein seized the pole and won the race... although he was later disqualified. Both Porsche and Nissan were penalized for technical infractions, for which Wehrlein's victory was annulled, as well as Lotterer's 16th place, Buemi's 18th and Rowland also suffered the penalty, although he had not made it out of the pits.

This situation was well used by Audi, with the Brazilian Lucas di Grassi returning to the top of the standings in a race and achieving a new victory, although far from the times in which he was fighting for championships. His partner René Rast was second.

Motoresapleno.com.ar

Third was the Swiss Edoardo Mortara for Venturi, with Vandoorne and Nyck de Vries finishing seventh and Evans eighth in the particular fight between Mercedes and Jaguar.

Puebla ePrix 2

For the second Mexican test, it was the British Oliver Rowland who achieved the pole trying to save the weekend for Nissan.

He was only able to hold the first position for four laps, until he was overtaken by Edoardo Mortara. The Swiss from Venturi managed to maintain the first position at the end of the race, achieving very good results in the races in Puebla.

Motoresapleno.com.ar

Second was the New Zealander Nick Cassidy, who returned to raise the Audi to a podium that was completed by Oliver Rowland, thus saving the Mexican event for Nissan.

Edoardo Mortara's two good races saw the Swiss lead the drivers 'championship, 10 points above Robin Frijns, while the Mercedes team held the top spot in the constructors' standings, now chased by DS Techeetah, who was just three points recovered and threatened to try to win the competition again.

New York ePrix 1

Audi's good performance continued in New York, with Nick Cassidy taking pole ahead of Vergne's Techeetah and Alex Lynn's Mahindra, who locked the wheels at the start dropping to fifth.

Cassidy was the last leading rider to activate attack mode, allowing him to continue to hold the top spot. The New Zealander was still chased by Vergne, and by Buemi in third place.

Cassidy kept up her fight with Vergne, who was joined in the latter part of the race by Günther, who had made very good use of energy, with all three drivers in less than two seconds. In the final part, Cassidy was left with less energy and Vergne also had the extra power granted by the fans, so he decided to go ahead, touching both in the maneuver. Günther took the opportunity to overtake both during the incident and take the lead in the race, with Vergne second and di Grassi third by stealing the spot from Cassidy.

Günther was able to keep the first position until the end to give the victory to BMW, with Vergne second and di Grassi third.

Soymotor.com

New York ePrix 2

In the second race in New York, Jaguar secured the first position for Sam Bird and the second for Mitch Evans on the starting grid with the aim of being able to continue fighting for the championship.

Bird made a great start and managed to distance himself in the early part of the race. His teammate Evans was also able to hold the second position, although he had to fight Cassidy for it.

Vergne's problems, who could not start the car at the start, caused the safety car to leave.

On lap 8, the two Jaguar drivers activated attack mode. Bird was able to keep the top position, but Cassidy took advantage of it to steal second place from Evans, who managed to regain his position later by taking advantage of the extra energy.

In the second activation of the attack mode, Cassidy and Evans once again overtook each other, but this fight allowed Da Costa to close in and snatch third place from the New Zealander.

Behind, the eternal rivals di Grassi and Buemi relived one of their legendary fights and ended up colliding. The Brazilian was penalized with 10 seconds.

Meanwhile, Cassidy and Da Costa had a tough fight for third place. Evans was trying to retain both (and the rest of the squad) so his teammate Bird could continue to enjoy more of the lead at the lead position.

However, Evans' strategy was not successful, he was overtaken by both Cassidy and Da Costa, descending to position number 13 finally.

Despite losing the help of his teammate, Sam Bird had no problem finishing the race to claim victory for Jaguar.

Motorsportweek.com

Nick Cassidy eventually beat Vergne, and they both completed the podium at the second New York race.

London ePrix 1

With only two double events to go, the championship came to London. For the first of two races in the Newham neighborhood, Briton Alex Lynn claimed pole position in his Mahindra, with Jake Dennis second on the starting grid in a standings led by the two local drivers.

At the start, Lynn held the first position against Dennis, with Buemi behind them.

At the end of the first lap, Sam Bird, who was leading the championship, was hit from behind and had to retire. His teammate Evans had to pit with damage to the rear wing, a fateful start for Jaguar in the constructors' championship.

The first part of the race happened without much change among the first drivers, but during the second activation of the attack mode, Dennis took the opportunity to snatch the first position from Lynn.

As Dennis managed to gain the advantage leading the race, Nyck de Vries took the opportunity to overtake Buemi and put the Mercedes in third position.

The British Jake Dennis did not have major complications until the end of the race, achieving victory for BMW and the second in his private account in his first season in the competition.

Grandprix247.com

With the help of the Fanboost, Nyck de Vries also managed to overtake Alex Lynn, which allowed him to finish second ahead of the Briton.

At the end of this race, Sam Bird was still leading the championship, but with only two points clear of Jake Dennis. Among the top five drivers, there were only five points of difference to an exciting season finale, with Techeetah and Virgin taking the top spots in the team standings.

London ePrix 2

In the second London race, it was the other Mercedes driver, Stoffel Vandoorne, who took pole ahead on the starting grid of Oliver Rowland and Alex Lynn who continued to put in a very good performance at home.

Vandoorne protected the first position at the start, to begin to gain an advantage over his followers. Meanwhile, Nyck de Vries overtook Lynn with the other Mercedes to place third.

Nissan driver Oliver Rowland was the first to activate attack mode looking to get ahead of the two Mercedes without much success.

With 35 minutes to go, Buemi's Nissan and Rene Rast's Audi suffered a severe accident that forced the safety car to be taken out.

After the restart, Nyck de Vries overtook Rowland getting the two Mercedes to lead the race.

On lap 11, the current champion Da Costa collided with Lotterer's Porsche, causing a new exit of the safety car that Lucas di Grassi took advantage of in a very clever way, entering the pits at the most favorable moment for him to start in first position .

Behind him, Rowland tried to overtake Vandoorne causing an accident for which he would be penalized that left both pilots out of the fight, handing the second position to Nyck de Vries, who also took advantage of the attack mode to overtake Lucas di Grassi and get the first position. In the latter part of the race, the Brazilian used the extra power of attack mode to regain first place.

Meanwhile, the championship leader, Sam Bird, had staged a great comeback taking 10 positions, but when he was fighting for some valuable points for the championship, he collided with Nato, leaving the two out of the race.

When di Grassi was already the winner, he was notified of his penalty for his inadequate passage through the pits, which allowed Alex Lynn to proclaim himself the winner of the race with his Mahindra.

Autoweek.com

De Vries finished second in the race, followed by Evans who achieved a podium that allowed Jaguar to continue fighting for the championship.

Berlin ePrix 1

In Berlin, a Formula E classic since the beginning of the championship, the last two races were held that ended up deciding the competition. The circuit was developed at Tempelhof Airport, using the original layout for race 1 and its inverted shape for race 2.

For the first race, the two DS Techeetah drivers (Vergne and Da Costa) took first and second positions on the starting grid. The Chinese team wanted to fight to the end to keep their championship title. The two drivers held their positions at the start and had a conservative start to the race, with Lucas di Grassi pressing behind them, less than a second apart between the three.

On lap 8, Sam Bird's Jaguar suffered from technical problems and the British driver lost many chances of winning the championship.

On lap 18, the two Techeetah drivers reversed positions, and Evans culminated a great comeback after overtaking Nato, Mortara, and Vergne himself reaching third position. Di Grassi also managed to overtake Vergne, with the two Audi drivers taking second and third positions, with Da Costa leading.

The Audi drivers continued to progress and both overtook Da Costa in a terrible final part of the race for Techeetah, as the Portuguese was also overtaken by Mortara.

So, the attack was by the Venturi team. Edoardo Mortara, taking advantage of the extra power of the attack mode, overtook the Audi drivers, something that his teammate Nato later replied.

Di Grassi did not give up and on lap 27 he overtook the two Venturi drivers to lead a spectacular race. Finally, the Brazilian achieved victory, putting Audi in the fight for the championship.

Motoresapleno.com.ar

The results of the first race in Berlin left a very tight classification that ensured a spectacular end of the season for the second German round.

More than half of the drivers in the championship still had options to be proclaimed champions before the last race. The Dutch Nyck de Vries led the standings with 95 points, just three ahead of the Swiss Edoardo Mortara, four from Jake Dennis and five from Mitch Evans.

Among the top seven finishers, which included Robin Frijns, Lucas Di Grassi and Da Costa, there were only 9 points difference.

Regarding the teams, Jaguar led the classification thanks to Evans' podium with only 5 points from the current champion, DS Techeetah, although the world was as open as the drivers, with teams with serious options to win the championship such as Mercedes, BMW, Virgin or Audi.

Berlin ePrix 2

In the last and exciting race of the season, Stoffel Vandoorne achieved pole position seeking to materialize Mercedes' chances of winning the championship. On the starting grid, he was followed by Oliver Rowland's Nissan and championship contender Mitch Evans' Jaguar, the top-ranked of the top four drivers in the overall standings. Paradoxically, the rest of the drivers with more possibilities had failed to qualify above 10th place, which gave Evans a great opportunity to become world champion.

However, Evans suffered a dramatic exit, where his Jaguar failed to start. Most of the pilots managed to avoid it, but Eduardo Mortara ended up colliding with him.

Both drivers, with options to be champions, were left out of the fight, and Jaguar also complicated the team championship.

Gruntstuff.com

After the red flag and the resumption of the race, it was Jake Dennis who had the best position to be world champion, something that he could achieve in his debut in the competition. However, a mistake caused him to crash against the wall and lose his great opportunity in the championship.

The one who remained in the mathematical position of champion after Dennis's accident was the Dutch Nyck de Vries, while the first position of Vandoorne made Mercedes also dream of the team championship.

In the first attack mode, Norman Nato took advantage and got the first place, while Vandoorne decided to activate it late and dropped to seventh position, complicating the possible Mercedes championship.

De Vries was still in eighth position, enough to be champion, but the two Mercedes drivers fought with Lotterer's Porsche when the three cars lined up, having contact between them and could have changed the situation of the championship drastically again, but luckily they were able to continue the race.

Meanwhile, Sam Bird, who had started in the 22nd position, was climbing to seventh place looking to score the necessary points for Jaguar to be proclaimed champion.

But it was not enough.

While the Frenchman Nato achieved his first victory in the competition, Nyck de Vries finished the race in eighth position and achieved four points that were enough to become world champion of Formula E.

Planetf1.com

Vandoorne, in addition, in a spectacular end of the race, managed to get on the podium, which allowed Mercedes to also achieve the team championship in its second year in the competition and in addition to reigning in Formula 1, it extended its success to electric competition. .

Autopista.es

The Swiss Edoardo Mortara managed to retain the runner-up in an exciting season and Jake Dennis confirmed his great debut with third place in the final classification. Mitch Evans, who started as a favorite before the green light in the last race, finished fourth.

The previous champion, Portuguese António Félix Da Costa, finished eighth, while legendary drivers of the competition such as Lucas di Grassi finished seventh and Sébastien Buemi 21st.

In terms of equipment, Mercedes achieved its goal of reigning in the competition in just two years. Jaguar closed a spectacular season that ended just 4 points behind the champion team.

Techeetah, who had won the previous season, had to settle for third and Audi, always competitive, was fourth.

BMW, Venturi, Porsche and Mahindra contested the middle of the standings, while Nissan e.Dams was far from its best years with Renault.

FINAL CLASSIFICATION 2021

Nyck de Vries	99	Mercedes-EQ Formula E Team	181
Edoardo Mortara	92	Jaguar Racing	177
Jake Dennis	91	DS Techeetah	166
Mitch Evans	90	Audi Sport ABT Schaeffler	165
Robin Frijns	89	Envision Virgin Racing	165
Sam Bird	87	BMW i Andretti Motorsport	157
Lucas di Grassi	87	ROKiT Venturi Racing	146
António Félix Da Costa	86	TAG Heuer Porsche	137
Stoffel Vandoorne	82	Mahindra Racing	132
Jean-Éric Vergne	80	Nissan e.Dams	97
Pascal Wehrlein	79	Dragon – Penske Autosport	47
Alex Lynn	78	NIO 333 FE Team	19
René Rast	78		
Oliver Rowland	77		
Nick Cassidy	76		
Maximilian Günther	66		
André Lotterer	58		
Norman Nato	54		
Alexander Sims	54		
Nico Müller	30		
Sébastien Buemi	20		
Sérgio Sette Camara	16		
Oliver Turkey	13		
Tom Blomqvist	6		
Joel Eriksson	1		

THANKS

To all of you who at some point in my life have connected with me and I with you through motorsport.

To all of you who have come across me around a circuit and have made me enjoy the roar of engines.

To all those who have helped me with this work, and to those who will continue to do so, appreciating any possible incorrectness.

To all the media whose graphic resources have been referred to in this work, for making it showy.

I hope you have enjoyed these pages and they have been useful to have a better understanding of the competition and enjoy it at a higher level.

Many thanks.
Chad Miller.

Printed in Great Britain
by Amazon